TIMELESS FOR SENIORS

:312 MULTIPLE-CHOICE TRIVIA QUESTIONS FOR SENIORS TO RELIVE THE ICONIC 50S-00S ERAS

FACTS MASTER

| SENIORS TRIVIA EDITION | Tabal of content | PAGE NO. 0 |

INTRODUCTION...**0**

1: NOSTALGIC NIFTIES: A BLAST FROM THE PAST..............**1**

2: THE SWINGIN' SIXTIES: A GROOVY TIME CAPSULE...........**14**

3: FUNKY SEVENTIES: A DECADE OF DISTINCTIVE VIBES......**27**

4: ELECTRIFYING EIGHTIES: NEON NOSTALGIA NIGHTS........**40**

5: GNARLY NINETIES: A RADICAL REMINISCENCE................**53**

6: MILLENNIAL MEMORIES: A NEW AGE NOSTALGIA TRIP....**66**

ANSWER..**79**

THE CONCLUSION..**82**

TIMELESS ✱ TRIVIA FOR ✱ SENIORS

Introduction

WELCOME TO TIMELESS TRIVIA FOR SENIORS: 312 MULTIPLE-CHOICE TRIVIA QUESTIONS FOR SENIORS TO RELIVE THE ICONIC 50S-00S ERAS. THIS BOOK CELEBRATES THE VIBRANT DECADES FROM THE 1950S TO THE EARLY 2000S, PERFECT FOR REMINISCING, CHALLENGING YOUR MEMORY, OR HAVING FUN.

INSIDE, YOU'LL FIND SIX CHAPTERS:NOSTALGIC NIFTIES: A BLAST FROM THE PAST1950S POP CULTURE, HISTORICAL EVENTS, AND CHERISHED MEMORIES.

THE SWINGIN' SIXTIES: A GROOVY TIME CAPSULE1960S MUSIC, FASHION, AND CULTURAL MOVEMENTS.FUNKY SEVENTIES: A DECADE OF DISTINCTIVE VIBES1970S UNIQUE VIBES, MUSIC, AND CULTURAL PHENOMENA.

ELECTRIFYING EIGHTIES: NEON NOSTALGIA NIGHTS1980S POP CULTURE, MUSIC VIDEOS, ICONIC FILMS, AND FASHION TRENDS.

GNARLY NINETIES: A RADICAL REMINISCENCE1990S TRENDS, EVENTS, AND CULTURAL SHIFTS.

MILLENNIAL MEMORIES: A NEW AGE NOSTALGIA TRIPEARLY 2000S CULTURAL MILESTONES AND NOSTALGIC MOMENTS.

EACH CHAPTER STARTS WITH A NOSTALGIC IMAGE. ANSWERS TO ALL TRIVIA QUESTIONS ARE AT THE END OF THE BOOK.WE HOPE THIS BOOK BRINGS BACK WONDERFUL MEMORIES AND PROVIDES HOURS OF ENJOYMENT. FOR MORE TRIVIA, SCAN THE QR CODE AT THE END OF THE BOOK TO EXPLORE OTHER TITLES BY FACTS MASTER. ENJOY!

TIMELESS ✽ TRIVIA FOR ✽ SENIORS

SENIORS TRIVIA EDITION

1: Nostalgic Nifties

1) WHICH POPULAR TOY WAS INTRODUCED IN THE 1950S?

A) TEDDY BEAR
B) RUBIK'S CUBE
C) HULA HOOP
D) ACTION MAN

2) IN WHICH U.S. STATE WAS THE FIRST MCDONALD'S RESTAURANT OPENED IN 1955?

A) CALIFORNIA
B) ILLINOIS
C) TEXAS
D) FLORIDA

3) WHO WAS THE FIRST AMERICAN TO WALK IN SPACE, IN 1965?

A) NEIL ARMSTRONG
B) BUZZ ALDRIN
C) JOHN GLENN
D) ED WHITE

4) WHICH AMERICAN AUTHOR'S NOVEL "FAHRENHEIT 451" WAS PUBLISHED IN 1953?

A) RAY BRADBURY
B) ISAAC ASIMOV
C) ARTHUR C. CLARKE
D) ROBERT A. HEINLEIN

TIMELESS ✱ TRIVIA FOR ✱ SENIORS

Nostalgic Trivia

SENIORS TRIVIA EDITION

5) WHO WAS THE U.S. PRESIDENT FOR MOST OF THE 1950S?

A) HARRY S. TRUMAN
B) RICHARD NIXON
C) DWIGHT D. EISENHOWER
D) JOHN F. KENNEDY

6) THE 1954 SUPREME COURT CASE, BROWN V. BOARD OF EDUCATION, DECLARED SEGREGATION IN PUBLIC SCHOOLS AS...?

A) CONSTITUTIONAL
B) UNCONSTITUTIONAL
C) A STATE'S CHOICE
D) A DISTRICT'S CHOICE

7) WHICH FAMOUS AMERICAN ARTIST'S WORKS, LIKE "CAMPBELL'S SOUP CANS," WERE POPULAR IN THE 1950S?

A) JACKSON POLLOCK
B) ANDY WARHOL
C) MARK ROTHKO
D) WILLEM DE KOONING

8) WHAT WAS THE NAME OF THE FIRST SUCCESSFUL LIVER TRANSPLANT, PERFORMED IN 1963?

A) STARZL
B) MURRAY
C) BARNARD
D) DEBAKEY

TIMELESS ✳ TRIVIA FOR ✳ SENIORS

Nostalgic Trivia

SENIORS TRIVIA EDITION

9) WHICH 1951 MOVIE STARRED MARLON BRANDO?

A) REAR WINDOW

B) A STREETCAR NAMED DESIRE

C) ON THE WATERFRONT

D) SUNSET BOULEVARD

10) WHICH CLASSIC 1950S SCI-FI FILM FEATURED AN ALIEN NAMED KLAATU?

A) INVASION OF THE BODY SNATCHERS

B) FORBIDDEN PLANET

C) THE DAY THE EARTH STOOD STILL

D) WAR OF THE WORLDS

11) WHAT WAS THE NAME OF THE FIRST SUCCESSFUL ARTIFICIAL HEART IMPLANTED IN A HUMAN IN 1982?

A) JARVIK-7

B) ABIOCOR

C) SYNCARDIA

D) HEARTMATE

12) WHICH ICONIC AMERICAN FILM ABOUT A TROUBLED TEENAGER WAS RELEASED IN 1955?

A) REBEL WITHOUT A CAUSE

B) THE WILD ONE

C) EAST OF EDEN

D) GIANT

TIMELESS ✼ TRIVIA FOR ✼ SENIORS

| SENIORS TRIVIA EDITION | **Nostalgic Trivia** | PAGE NO. 4 |

13) WHICH ARTIST IS KNOWN AS THE "KING OF ROCK AND ROLL"?

A) CHUCK BERRY

B) JOHNNY CASH

C) ELVIS PRESLEY

D) BUDDY HOLLY

14) WHAT TYPE OF MUSIC, ROOTED IN AFRICAN-AMERICAN COMMUNITIES OF NEW ORLEANS, GAINED IMMENSE POPULARITY IN THE 1950S?

A) SWING

B) JAZZ

C) ROCK 'N' ROLL

D) BLUES

15) WHICH ICONIC AMERICAN NOVEL ABOUT THE SALEM WITCH TRIALS WAS PUBLISHED IN 1953?

A) THE GRAPES OF WRATH

B) THE CATCHER IN THE RYE

C) THE CRUCIBLE

D) TO KILL A MOCKINGBIRD

16) WHAT WAS THE NAME OF THE FIRST SUCCESSFUL LUNG TRANSPLANT, PERFORMED IN 1963?

A) HARDY

B) COOPER

C) BARNARD

D) STARZL

TIMELESS ✸ TRIVIA FOR ✸ SENIORS

17) IN 1954, ROGER BANNISTER ACHIEVED WHAT SPORTING MILESTONE?

A) SCORED 100 GOALS IN A SOCCER SEASON

B) SWAM THE ENGLISH CHANNEL

C) RAN A MILE IN UNDER FOUR MINUTES

D) WON FIVE GOLD MEDALS IN THE OLYMPICS

18) WHICH AUTOMOBILE COMPANY INTRODUCED THE "THUNDERBIRD" MODEL IN THE 1950S?

A) CHEVROLET

B) CHRYSLER

C) FORD

D) DODGE

19) WHAT WAS THE NAME OF THE FIRST SUCCESSFUL POLIO VACCINE, INTRODUCED IN 1955?

A) SALK VACCINE

B) SABIN VACCINE

C) JENNER VACCINE

D) PASTEUR VACCINE

20) WHICH AMERICAN MUSICIAN'S ALBUM "THE FABULOUS JOHNNY CASH" WAS RELEASED IN 1958?

A) ELVIS PRESLEY

B) JOHNNY CASH

C) BUDDY HOLLY

D) CHUCK BERRY

TIMELESS ✸ TRIVIA FOR ✸ SENIORS

Nostalgic Trivia

SENIORS TRIVIA EDITION

21) WHICH TV SHOW, PREMIERING IN 1951, STARRED LUCILLE BALL?

A) THE TWILIGHT ZONE
B) THE ED SULLIVAN SHOW
C) THE BEVERLY HILLBILLIES
D) I LOVE LUCY

22) WHO FAMOUSLY SAID, "IN THE FUTURE, EVERYONE WILL BE WORLD-FAMOUS FOR 15 MINUTES," DURING THE 1950S?

A) FRANK SINATRA
B) MARILYN MONROE
C) JOHN F. KENNEDY
D) ANDY WARHOL

23) WHICH AMERICAN JAZZ MUSICIAN WAS KNOWN AS THE "KING OF SWING"?

A) DUKE ELLINGTON
B) LOUIS ARMSTRONG
C) BENNY GOODMAN
D) COUNT BASIE

24) WHAT WAS THE NAME OF THE FIRST SUCCESSFUL ARTIFICIAL HEART VALVE, DEVELOPED IN 1960?

A) STARR-EDWARDS
B) ST. JUDE MEDICAL
C) MEDTRONIC
D) EDWARDS LIFESCIENCES

TIMELESS TRIVIA FOR SENIORS

Nostalgic Trivia

SENIORS TRIVIA EDITION

PAGE NO. 7

25) IN 1953, SIR EDMUND HILLARY AND TENZING NORGAY BECAME THE FIRST TO...?

A) CROSS THE ATLANTIC IN A BALLOON
B) CLIMB MOUNT EVEREST
C) SAIL AROUND THE WORLD
D) REACH THE SOUTH POLE

26) WHICH ACTRESS STARRED ALONGSIDE HUMPHREY BOGART IN THE 1951 FILM "THE AFRICAN QUEEN"?

A) LAUREN BACALL
B) AUDREY HEPBURN
C) KATHARINE HEPBURN
D) BETTE DAVIS

27) WHAT WAS THE NAME OF THE FIRST SUCCESSFUL ORGAN TRANSPLANT, PERFORMED IN 1954?

A) HEART
B) KIDNEY
C) LIVER
D) LUNG

28) WHICH ICONIC AMERICAN FILM ABOUT A YOUNG BOXER WAS RELEASED IN 1949?

A) ON THE WATERFRONT
B) THE HUSTLER
C) RAGING BULL
D) ROCKY

TIMELESS ✱ TRIVIA FOR ✱ SENIORS

Nostalgic Trivia

SENIORS TRIVIA EDITION — PAGE NO. 8

---

29) WHICH DISNEY THEME PARK OPENED IN 1955?

A) DISNEY WORLD

B) EPCOT

C) DISNEYLAND

D) DISNEY'S HOLLYWOOD STUDIOS

---

30) WHO WAS THE ORIGINAL HOST OF THE 1950S QUIZ SHOW "THE $64,000 QUESTION"?

A) HAL MARCH

B) JACK BARRY

C) BILL CULLEN

D) BOB BARKER

---

31) WHICH ICONIC AMERICAN MUSICAL FILM STARRED GENE KELLY AND WAS RELEASED IN 1952?

A) SINGIN' IN THE RAIN

B) THE WIZARD OF OZ

C) WEST SIDE STORY

D) THE SOUND OF MUSIC

---

32) WHAT WAS THE NAME OF THE FIRST SUCCESSFUL KIDNEY TRANSPLANT, PERFORMED IN 1954?

A) MURRAY

B) STARZL

C) BARNARD

D) HARDY

TIMELESS ✱ TRIVIA FOR ✱ SENIORS

Nostalgic Trivia
SENIORS TRIVIA EDITION

33) WHICH OF THESE CAR MODELS BECAME AN ICON OF THE 1950S?

A) MODEL T FORD
B) VOLKSWAGEN BEETLE
C) CHEVROLET CORVETTE
D) HONDA CIVIC

34) WHICH ICONIC HOLLYWOOD ACTRESS WAS KNOWN AS THE "BLONDE BOMBSHELL" IN THE 1950S?

A) AUDREY HEPBURN
B) MARILYN MONROE
C) GRACE KELLY
D) ELIZABETH TAYLOR

35) WHAT WAS THE NAME OF THE FIRST SUCCESSFUL ARTIFICIAL PACEMAKER, IMPLANTED IN 1958?

A) CHARDACK-GREATBATCH
B) MEDTRONIC
C) ST. JUDE MEDICAL
D) BOSTON SCIENTIFIC

36) WHICH AMERICAN MUSICIAN'S ALBUM "THE BUDDY HOLLY STORY" WAS RELEASED IN 1959?

A) ELVIS PRESLEY
B) JOHNNY CASH
C) BUDDY HOLLY
D) CHUCK BERRY

TIMELESS ✱ TRIVIA FOR ✱ SENIORS

Nostalgic Trivia

37) WHICH NOVEL, WRITTEN BY J.D. SALINGER AND PUBLISHED IN 1951, BECAME AN IMMEDIATE CLASSIC?

A) ON THE ROAD

B) TO KILL A MOCKINGBIRD

C) BRAVE NEW WORLD

D) THE CATCHER IN THE RYE

38) WHAT WAS THE NAME OF THE FIRST SATELLITE LAUNCHED INTO ORBIT IN 1957?

A) SPUTNIK 1

B) EXPLORER 1

C) VANGUARD 1

D) TELSTAR 1

39) WHICH AMERICAN AUTHOR'S NOVEL "THE OLD MAN AND THE SEA" WAS PUBLISHED IN 1951?

A) JOHN STEINBECK

B) ERNEST HEMINGWAY

C) F. SCOTT FITZGERALD

D) WILLIAM FAULKNER

40) WHAT WAS THE NAME OF THE FIRST SUCCESSFUL PANCREAS TRANSPLANT, PERFORMED IN 1966?

A) KELLY

B) LILLEHEI

C) STARZL

D) BARNARD

TIMELESS ✷ TRIVIA FOR ✷ SENIORS

Nostalgic Trivia

SENIORS TRIVIA EDITION

41) WHICH ICONIC ACTOR STARRED AS A TROUBLED REBEL IN THE 1955 FILM "REBEL WITHOUT A CAUSE"?

- A) MARLON BRANDO
- B) PAUL NEWMAN
- C) JAMES DEAN
- D) CARY GRANT

42) WHICH AMERICAN PLAYWRIGHT'S WORKS LIKE "A STREETCAR NAMED DESIRE" AND "CAT ON A HOT TIN ROOF" WERE POPULAR IN THE 1950S?

- A) ARTHUR MILLER
- B) TENNESSEE WILLIAMS
- C) EUGENE O'NEILL
- D) EDWARD ALBEE

43) WHAT WAS THE NAME OF THE FIRST SUCCESSFUL WEATHER SATELLITE, LAUNCHED IN 1960?

- A) TIROS-1
- B) VANGUARD 2
- C) EXPLORER 1
- D) SPUTNIK 1

44) WHICH ICONIC AMERICAN FILM ABOUT A YOUNG BOXER WAS RELEASED IN 1976?

- A) ON THE WATERFRONT
- B) THE HUSTLER
- C) RAGING BULL
- D) ROCKY

TIMELESS ✳ TRIVIA FOR ✳ SENIORS

45) WHICH GROUNDBREAKING 1950S TV SHOW WAS SET IN NEW YORK AND FOCUSED ON A CUBAN BANDLEADER AND HIS WIFE?

A) THE HONEYMOONERS

B) I LOVE LUCY

C) THE PERRY COMO SHOW

D) THE JACK BENNY PROGRAM

46) WHAT WAS THE NAME OF THE FIRST NUCLEAR-POWERED SUBMARINE, LAUNCHED IN 1954?

A) USS NAUTILUS

B) USS ENTERPRISE

C) USS NIMITZ

D) USS STENNIS

47) WHICH ICONIC AMERICAN COMEDIAN HOSTED THE POPULAR TV SHOW "THE ED SULLIVAN SHOW" IN THE 1950S?

A) BOB HOPE

B) JERRY SEINFELD

C) ED SULLIVAN

D) JOHNNY CARSON

48) WHAT WAS THE NAME OF THE FIRST SUCCESSFUL HEART-LUNG TRANSPLANT, PERFORMED IN 1981?

A) SHUMWAY

B) COOPER

C) BARNARD

D) STARZL

Nostalgic Trivia

SENIORS TRIVIA EDITION

PAGE NO. 13

49) WHICH OF THESE WAS NOT A POPULAR 1950S DANCE?

A) THE TWIST
B) THE JITTERBUG
C) THE MASHED POTATO
D) THE WALTZ

50) WHICH ICONIC SCIENCE FICTION FILM ABOUT A MASSIVE INSECT INVASION WAS RELEASED IN 1954?

A) INVASION OF THE BODY SNATCHERS
B) THEM!
C) THE THING FROM ANOTHER WORLD
D) THE DAY THE EARTH STOOD STILL

51) WHAT WAS THE NAME OF THE FIRST SUCCESSFUL HEART TRANSPLANT, PERFORMED IN 1967?

A) BARNARD
B) DEBAKEY
C) COOLEY
D) SHUMWAY

52) WHICH AMERICAN MUSICIAN'S ALBUM "THE GREAT TWENTY-EIGHT" WAS RELEASED IN 1958?

A) ELVIS PRESLEY
B) JOHNNY CASH
C) BUDDY HOLLY
D) CHUCK BERRY

TIMELESS * TRIVIA FOR * SENIORS

SENIORS TRIVIA EDITION

2: The Swingin' Sixties

1) WHICH ICONIC FASHION ITEM BECAME A SYMBOL OF THE 1960S COUNTERCULTURE MOVEMENT?

A) BELL-BOTTOMS
B) MINISKIRTS
C) TIE-DYE SHIRTS
D) ALL OF THE ABOVE

2) WHICH ICONIC 1960S TV SHOW FEATURED A FAMILY LIVING ON A COLONY IN SPACE?

A) STAR TREK
B) THE JETSONS
C) LOST IN SPACE
D) MY FAVORITE MARTIAN

3) WHAT WAS THE NAME OF THE FIRST SUCCESSFUL ARTIFICIAL HEART VALVE, DEVELOPED IN 1960?

A) STARR-EDWARDS
B) ST. JUDE MEDICAL
C) MEDTRONIC
D) EDWARDS LIFESCIENCES

4) WHICH ICONIC 1960S FILM STARRED PETER O'TOOLE AS A FLAMBOYANT ENGLISH TEACHER?

A) GOODBYE, MR. CHIPS
B) TO SIR, WITH LOVE
C) THE PRIME OF MISS JEAN BRODIE
D) BLACKBOARD JUNGLE

TIMELESS ✳ TRIVIA FOR ✳ SENIORS

| SENIORS TRIVIA EDITION | **Nostalgic Trivia** | PAGE NO. 15 |

5) WHO WAS THE FIRST AMERICAN TO WALK ON THE MOON IN 1969?

A) BUZZ ALDRIN
B) NEIL ARMSTRONG
C) MICHAEL COLLINS
D) ALAN SHEPARD

6) WHAT WAS THE NAME OF THE FIRST SUCCESSFUL MANNED MISSION TO LAND ON THE MOON IN 1969?

A) APOLLO 11
B) APOLLO 13
C) GEMINI 5
D) MERCURY 7

7) WHICH ICONIC 1960S FILM STARRED WARREN BEATTY AND FAYE DUNAWAY AS BANK ROBBERS?

A) BONNIE AND CLYDE
B) THE GETAWAY
C) THE THOMAS CROWN AFFAIR
D) BUTCH CASSIDY AND THE SUNDANCE KID

8) WHO WAS THE FAMOUS FOLK SINGER KNOWN FOR SONGS LIKE "BLOWIN' IN THE WIND" AND "THE TIMES THEY ARE A-CHANGIN'"?

A) JOAN BAEZ
B) BOB DYLAN
C) PETE SEEGER
D) WOODY GUTHRIE

TIMELESS ✳ TRIVIA FOR ✳ SENIORS

Nostalgic Trivia

SENIORS TRIVIA EDITION

9) WHAT WAS THE NAME OF THE LEGENDARY MUSIC FESTIVAL HELD IN 1969 IN BETHEL, NEW YORK?

A) LOLLAPALOOZA
B) COACHELLA
C) WOODSTOCK
D) BONNAROO

10) WHICH ICONIC 1960S FILM STARRED DUSTIN HOFFMAN AS A YOUNG COLLEGE GRADUATE?

A) THE GRADUATE
B) MIDNIGHT COWBOY
C) EASY RIDER
D) BONNIE AND CLYDE

11) WHO WAS THE FAMOUS SINGER KNOWN AS THE "FIRST LADY OF SONG" WHO ROSE TO FAME IN THE 1960S?

A) ELLA FITZGERALD
B) BILLIE HOLIDAY
C) SARAH VAUGHAN
D) ETTA JAMES

12) WHICH ICONIC 1960S TV SHOW FEATURED A FAMILY LIVING IN A SUBURBAN NEIGHBORHOOD WITH A NOSY NEIGHBOR?

A) BEWITCHED
B) I DREAM OF JEANNIE
C) THE ADDAMS FAMILY
D) THE MUNSTERS

TIMELESS � TRIVIA FOR ✻ SENIORS

Nostalgic Trivia

SENIORS TRIVIA EDITION

13) WHICH ICONIC 1960S FILM STARRED AUDREY HEPBURN AS A QUIRKY NEW YORK SOCIALITE?

A) BREAKFAST AT TIFFANY'S
B) ROMAN HOLIDAY
C) CHARADE
D) SABRINA

14) WHO WAS THE FAMOUS SINGER KNOWN AS THE "KING OF ROCK AND ROLL" WHO DIED IN 1977?

A) CHUCK BERRY
B) BUDDY HOLLY
C) ELVIS PRESLEY
D) JERRY LEE LEWIS

15) WHICH ICONIC 1960S TV SHOW FEATURED A FAMILY LIVING IN A PREHISTORIC AGE?

A) THE FLINTSTONES
B) THE JETSONS
C) THE BEVERLY HILLBILLIES
D) GILLIGAN'S ISLAND

16) WHAT WAS THE NAME OF THE FIRST SUCCESSFUL LUNG TRANSPLANT, PERFORMED IN 1963?

A) HARDY
B) COOPER
C) BARNARD
D) STARZL

TIMELESS ✻ TRIVIA FOR ✻ SENIORS

SENIORS TRIVIA EDITION

Nostalgic Trivia

PAGE NO. 18

---

17) WHO WAS THE LEADER OF THE CIVIL RIGHTS MOVEMENT AND DELIVERED THE FAMOUS "I HAVE A DREAM" SPEECH IN 1963?

A) MALCOLM X

B) ROSA PARKS

C) MARTIN LUTHER KING JR.

D) MEDGAR EVERS

---

18) WHICH ICONIC 1960S TV SHOW FEATURED A FAMILY LIVING IN A HAUNTED MANSION?

A) THE MUNSTERS

B) THE ADDAMS FAMILY

C) DARK SHADOWS

D) TWIN PEAKS

---

19) WHAT WAS THE NAME OF THE FIRST SUCCESSFUL ARTIFICIAL HEART IMPLANTED IN A HUMAN IN 1982?

A) JARVIK-7

B) ABIOCOR

C) SYNCARDIA

D) HEARTMATE

---

20) WHICH ICONIC 1960S FILM STARRED JANE FONDA AND DONALD SUTHERLAND AS FREE-SPIRITED HIPPIES?

A) EASY RIDER

B) THE TRIP

C) ALICE'S RESTAURANT

D) ZABRISKIE POINT

TIMELESS ✻ TRIVIA FOR ✻ SENIORS

Nostalgic Trivia

SENIORS TRIVIA EDITION

21) WHICH ICONIC 1960S TV SHOW FEATURED A FAMILY LIVING IN A SUBURBAN UTOPIA?

A) THE BRADY BUNCH

B) THE FLINTSTONES

C) LEAVE IT TO BEAVER

D) THE ADDAMS FAMILY

22) WHAT WAS THE NAME OF THE FIRST SUCCESSFUL HEART-LUNG TRANSPLANT, PERFORMED IN 1981?

A) SHUMWAY

B) COOPER

C) BARNARD

D) STARZL

23) WHICH ICONIC 1960S FILM STARRED SIDNEY POITIER AS A PHILADELPHIA DETECTIVE?

A) IN THE HEAT OF THE NIGHT

B) GUESS WHO'S COMING TO DINNER

C) TO SIR, WITH LOVE

D) A RAISIN IN THE SUN

24) WHO WAS THE FAMOUS SINGER KNOWN AS THE "QUEEN OF GOSPEL" WHO ROSE TO FAME IN THE 1960S?

A) MAHALIA JACKSON

B) ARETHA FRANKLIN

C) ETTA JAMES

D) MAVIS STAPLES

TIMELESS ✳ TRIVIA FOR ✳ SENIORS

SENIORS TRIVIA EDITION

Nostalgic Trivia

PAGE NO. 20

---

25) WHAT WAS THE NAME OF THE FIRST SUCCESSFUL ORAL CONTRACEPTIVE PILL APPROVED FOR USE IN 1960?

A) THE PILL

B) BIRTH CONTROL PILL

C) ENOVID

D) ORTHO-NOVUM

---

26) WHICH ICONIC 1960S FILM STARRED STEVE MCQUEEN AS A COOL POLICE DETECTIVE?

A) BULLITT

B) THE THOMAS CROWN AFFAIR

C) THE FRENCH CONNECTION

D) DIRTY HARRY

---

27) WHO WAS THE FAMOUS SINGER KNOWN AS THE "PRINCE OF MOTOWN" WHO ROSE TO FAME IN THE 1960S?

A) MARVIN GAYE

B) STEVIE WONDER

C) SMOKEY ROBINSON

D) THE TEMPTATIONS

---

28) WHICH ICONIC 1960S TV SHOW FEATURED A SINGLE MOTHER RAISING HER THREE DAUGHTERS?

A) THE PARTRIDGE FAMILY

B) THE BRADY BUNCH

C) THE DONNA REED SHOW

D) THAT GIRL

TIMELESS ✱ TRIVIA FOR ✱ SENIORS

29) WHICH ICONIC 1960S FILM STARRED JULIE ANDREWS AS A BELOVED NANNY?

A) THE SOUND OF MUSIC

B) MARY POPPINS

C) CHITTY CHITTY BANG BANG

D) BEDKNOBS AND BROOMSTICKS

30) WHO WAS THE FAMOUS SINGER KNOWN AS THE "KING OF POP" WHO ROSE TO FAME AS A CHILD STAR IN THE 1960S?

A) MICHAEL JACKSON

B) PRINCE

C) STEVIE WONDER

D) MARVIN GAYE

31) WHICH ICONIC 1960S TV SHOW FEATURED A FAMILY LIVING ON AN ISLAND AFTER A SHIPWRECK?

A) GILLIGAN'S ISLAND

B) FANTASY ISLAND

C) THE LOVE BOAT

D) MAGNUM P.I.

32) WHAT WAS THE NAME OF THE FIRST SUCCESSFUL PANCREAS TRANSPLANT, PERFORMED IN 1966?

A) KELLY

B) LILLEHEI

C) STARZL

D) BARNARD

TIMELESS ✷ TRIVIA FOR ✷ SENIORS

SENIORS TRIVIA EDITION

Nostalgic Trivia

---

33) WHO WAS THE FAMOUS BOXER KNOWN AS "THE GREATEST" WHO CONVERTED TO ISLAM IN THE 1960S?

A) JOE FRAZIER

B) GEORGE FOREMAN

C) MUHAMMAD ALI

D) MIKE TYSON

---

34) WHICH ICONIC 1960S TV SHOW FEATURED A TALKING CAR NAMED KITT?

A) THE DUKES OF HAZZARD

B) KNIGHT RIDER

C) THE A-TEAM

D) MAGNUM P.I.

---

35) WHAT WAS THE NAME OF THE FIRST SUCCESSFUL KIDNEY TRANSPLANT, PERFORMED IN 1954?

A) MURRAY

B) STARZL

C) BARNARD

D) HARDY

---

36) WHICH ICONIC 1960S FILM STARRED ELIZABETH TAYLOR AND RICHARD BURTON AS A MARRIED COUPLE IN A TUMULTUOUS RELATIONSHIP?

A) WHO'S AFRAID OF VIRGINIA WOOLF?

B) CAT ON A HOT TIN ROOF

C) CLEOPATRA

D) THE TAMING OF THE SHREW

TIMELESS ✼ TRIVIA FOR ✼ SENIORS

Nostalgic Trivia

Seniors Trivia Edition

37) WHICH ICONIC 1960S TV SHOW FEATURED A SECRET AGENT WHO LOVED MARTINIS?

A) GET SMART
B) THE MAN FROM U.N.C.L.E.
C) THE AVENGERS
D) JAMES BOND

38) WHAT WAS THE NAME OF THE FIRST SUCCESSFUL ARTIFICIAL HEART IMPLANTED IN A HUMAN IN 1982?

A) JARVIK-7
B) ABIOCOR
C) SYNCARDIA
D) HEARTMATE

39) WHICH ICONIC 1960S FILM STARRED PETER SELLERS AS MULTIPLE CHARACTERS IN A COMEDIC SPY CAPER?

A) THE PINK PANTHER
B) DR. STRANGELOVE
C) THE PARTY
D) CASINO ROYALE

40) WHO WAS THE FAMOUS SINGER KNOWN AS THE "PEARL OF DETROIT" WHO ROSE TO FAME IN THE 1960S?

A) DIANA ROSS
B) MARTHA REEVES
C) MARY WELLS
D) GLADYS KNIGHT

TIMELESS ✱ TRIVIA FOR ✱ SENIORS

Nostalgic Trivia
SENIORS TRIVIA EDITION

41) WHAT WAS THE NAME OF THE FIRST SUCCESSFUL HUMAN HEART TRANSPLANT, PERFORMED IN 1967?

A) BARNARD
B) DEBAKEY
C) COOLEY
D) SHUMWAY

42) WHICH ICONIC 1960S FILM STARRED JANE FONDA AS A SEX SYMBOL AND SPACE TRAVELER?

A) BARBARELLA
B) FANTASTIC VOYAGE
C) PLANET OF THE APES
D) 2001: A SPACE ODYSSEY

43) WHO WAS THE FAMOUS SINGER KNOWN AS THE "FIRST LADY OF ROCK" WHO ROSE TO FAME IN THE 1960S?

A) TINA TURNER
B) JANIS JOPLIN
C) CHER
D) ARETHA FRANKLIN

44) WHICH ICONIC 1960S TV SHOW FEATURED A FAMILY LIVING IN A SUBURBAN NEIGHBORHOOD WITH A WACKY NEIGHBOR?

A) THE MUNSTERS
B) BEWITCHED
C) THE ADDAMS FAMILY
D) THE BRADY BUNCH

TIMELESS ✶ TRIVIA FOR ✶ SENIORS

| SENIORS TRIVIA EDITION | **Nostalgic Trivia** | PAGE NO. 25 |

45) WHICH ICONIC 1960S FILM STARRED PAUL NEWMAN AND ROBERT REDFORD AS CON MEN?

A) THE STING

B) BUTCH CASSIDY AND THE SUNDANCE KID

C) THE GREAT ESCAPE

D) COOL HAND LUKE

46) WHO WAS THE FAMOUS SINGER KNOWN AS THE "QUEEN OF ROCK" WHO ROSE TO FAME IN THE 1960S?

A) JANIS JOPLIN

B) TINA TURNER

C) CHER

D) JOAN BAEZ

47) WHICH ICONIC 1960S TV SHOW FEATURED A SUBURBAN FAMILY WITH TWO YOUNG SONS?

A) THE PARTRIDGE FAMILY

B) THE BRADY BUNCH

C) LEAVE IT TO BEAVER

D) THE DONNA REED SHOW

48) WHAT WAS THE NAME OF THE FIRST SUCCESSFUL ARTIFICIAL HEART IMPLANTED IN A HUMAN IN 1982?

A) JARVIK-7

B) ABIOCOR

C) SYNCARDIA

D) HEARTMATE

TIMELESS ✻ TRIVIA FOR ✻ SENIORS

SENIORS TRIVIA EDITION

Nostalgic Trivia

49) WHO WAS THE FAMOUS SINGER KNOWN AS THE "QUEEN OF SOUL" WHO ROSE TO FAME IN THE 1960S?

A) TINA TURNER

B) ARETHA FRANKLIN

C) DIANA ROSS

D) JANIS JOPLIN

50) WHICH ICONIC 1960S TV SHOW FEATURED A FAMILY LIVING IN A FUTURISTIC HOME WITH ADVANCED TECHNOLOGY?

A) THE JETSONS

B) THE FLINTSTONES

C) BEWITCHED

D) I DREAM OF JEANNIE

51) WHAT WAS THE NAME OF THE FIRST SUCCESSFUL LIVER TRANSPLANT, PERFORMED IN 1963?

A) STARZL

B) MURRAY

C) BARNARD

D) DEBAKEY

52) WHICH ICONIC 1960S FILM STARRED ROD STEIGER AS A SOUTHERN POLICE CHIEF DEALING WITH A MURDER CASE?

A) IN THE HEAT OF THE NIGHT

B) TO KILL A MOCKINGBIRD

C) MISSISSIPPI BURNING

D) A TIME TO KILL

TIMELESS ✳ TRIVIA FOR ✳ SENIORS

SENIORS TRIVIA EDITION **3: Funky Seventies**

1) WHICH ICONIC 1970S FILM STARRED ROBERT DE NIRO AS A YOUNG VITO CORLEONE?

- A) THE GODFATHER PART II
- B) THE GODFATHER
- C) SERPICO
- D) MEAN STREETS

2) WHO WAS THE FAMOUS SINGER KNOWN AS THE "PRINCE OF MOTOWN" WHO ROSE TO FAME IN THE 1960S AND CONTINUED SUCCESS IN THE 1970S?

- A) MARVIN GAYE
- B) STEVIE WONDER
- C) SMOKEY ROBINSON
- D) THE TEMPTATIONS

3) WHICH ICONIC 1970S TV SHOW FEATURED A GROUP OF POLICE OFFICERS IN A PRECINCT IN LOS ANGELES?

- A) BARNEY MILLER
- B) HILL STREET BLUES
- C) STARSKY & HUTCH
- D) DRAGNET

4) WHAT WAS THE NAME OF THE FIRST SUCCESSFUL ARTIFICIAL HEART IMPLANTED IN A HUMAN IN 1982?

- A) JARVIK-7
- B) ABIOCOR
- C) SYNCARDIA
- D) HEARTMATE

TIMELESS ✷ TRIVIA FOR ✷ SENIORS

SENIORS TRIVIA EDITION

Nostalgic Trivia

5) WHO WAS THE FAMOUS SINGER KNOWN AS THE "QUEEN OF DISCO" WHO ROSE TO FAME IN THE 1970S?

A) DONNA SUMMER

B) GLORIA GAYNOR

C) CHAKA KHAN

D) DIANA ROSS

6) WHICH ICONIC 1970S TV SHOW FEATURED A GROUP OF POLICE OFFICERS IN A PRECINCT IN NEW YORK CITY?

A) BARNEY MILLER

B) HILL STREET BLUES

C) NYPD BLUE

D) CAGNEY & LACEY

7) WHAT WAS THE NAME OF THE FIRST SUCCESSFUL LUNG TRANSPLANT, PERFORMED IN 1963?

A) HARDY

B) COOPER

C) BARNARD

D) STARZL

8) WHICH ICONIC 1970S FILM STARRED BARBRA STREISAND AS A SINGER WHO BECOMES INVOLVED WITH A POLITICIAN?

A) A STAR IS BORN

B) FUNNY GIRL

C) THE WAY WE WERE

D) YENTL

TIMELESS � TRIVIA FOR � SENIORS

9) WHICH ICONIC 1970S TV SHOW FEATURED A GROUP OF WORKING-CLASS FRIENDS IN A BOSTON BAR?

A) CHEERS

B) MAS*H

C) ALL IN THE FAMILY

D) THE MARY TYLER MOORE SHOW

10) WHAT WAS THE NAME OF THE FIRST SUCCESSFUL PANCREAS TRANSPLANT, PERFORMED IN 1966?

A) KELLY

B) LILLEHEI

C) STARZL

D) BARNARD

11) WHICH ICONIC 1970S FILM STARRED SYLVESTER STALLONE AS A BOXER FROM PHILADELPHIA?

A) ROCKY

B) RAGING BULL

C) THE CHAMP

D) BODY AND SOUL

12) WHO WAS THE FAMOUS SINGER KNOWN AS THE "MIGHTY BURNER" WHO ROSE TO FAME IN THE 1970S?

A) MICHAEL JACKSON

B) MARVIN GAYE

C) STEVIE WONDER

D) DONNY HATHAWAY

Nostalgic Trivia

SENIORS TRIVIA EDITION

13) WHAT WAS THE NAME OF THE FIRST SUCCESSFUL ARTIFICIAL HEART VALVE, DEVELOPED IN 1960?

A) STARR-EDWARDS

B) ST. JUDE MEDICAL

C) MEDTRONIC

D) EDWARDS LIFESCIENCES

14) WHICH ICONIC 1970S FILM STARRED ROY SCHEIDER AS A POLICE CHIEF DEALING WITH A KILLER SHARK?

A) JAWS

B) THE STING

C) THE EXORCIST

D) THE GODFATHER

15) WHO WAS THE FAMOUS SINGER KNOWN AS THE "QUEEN OF COUNTRY MUSIC" WHO ROSE TO FAME IN THE 1970S?

A) DOLLY PARTON

B) LORETTA LYNN

C) TAMMY WYNETTE

D) PATSY CLINE

16) WHICH ICONIC 1970S TV SHOW FEATURED A GROUP OF POLICE OFFICERS IN A PRECINCT IN NEW YORK CITY?

A) BARNEY MILLER

B) HILL STREET BLUES

C) NYPD BLUE

D) MCCLOUD

TIMELESS ✳ TRIVIA FOR ✳ SENIORS

Nostalgic Trivia

SENIORS TRIVIA EDITION

17) WHICH ICONIC 1970S FILM STARRED DUSTIN HOFFMAN AS AN UNCONVENTIONAL ACTOR?

A) TOOTSIE
B) THE GRADUATE
C) RAIN MAN
D) KRAMER VS. KRAMER

18) WHO WAS THE FAMOUS SINGER KNOWN AS THE "QUEEN OF FUNK" WHO ROSE TO FAME IN THE 1970S?

A) CHAKA KHAN
B) DONNA SUMMER
C) GLORIA GAYNOR
D) TINA TURNER

19) WHICH ICONIC 1970S TV SHOW FEATURED A GROUP OF WOMEN WORKING AS PRIVATE INVESTIGATORS?

A) CHARLIE'S ANGELS
B) POLICE WOMAN
C) CAGNEY & LACEY
D) THE ROOKIES

20) WHAT WAS THE NAME OF THE FIRST SUCCESSFUL HEART-LUNG TRANSPLANT, PERFORMED IN 1981?

A) SHUMWAY
B) COOPER
C) BARNARD
D) STARZL

TIMELESS ✶ TRIVIA FOR ✶ SENIORS

SENIORS TRIVIA EDITION

Nostalgic Trivia

PAGENO. 32

21) WHO WAS THE FAMOUS SINGER KNOWN AS THE "GODFATHER OF SOUL" WHO ROSE TO FAME IN THE 1970S?

A) JAMES BROWN

B) MARVIN GAYE

C) STEVIE WONDER

D) AL GREEN

22) WHICH ICONIC 1970S TV SHOW FEATURED A FAMILY LIVING IN A WEALTHY NEIGHBORHOOD IN CALIFORNIA?

A) THE BRADY BUNCH

B) THE PARTRIDGE FAMILY

C) THE WALTONS

D) BEVERLY HILLS, 90210

23) WHAT WAS THE NAME OF THE FIRST SUCCESSFUL ARTIFICIAL HEART IMPLANTED IN A HUMAN IN 1982?

A) JARVIK-7

B) ABIOCOR

C) SYNCARDIA

D) HEARTMATE

24) WHICH ICONIC 1970S FILM STARRED RICHARD DREYFUSS AS A MAN WHO BECOMES OBSESSED WITH UFOS?

A) CLOSE ENCOUNTERS OF THE THIRD KIND

B) STAR WARS

C) E.T. THE EXTRA-TERRESTRIAL

D) ALIEN

TIMELESS ✱ TRIVIA FOR ✱ SENIORS

Nostalgic Trivia

25) WHICH ICONIC 1970S TV SHOW FEATURED A GROUP OF MOBILE ARMY SURGICAL HOSPITAL STAFF DURING THE KOREAN WAR?

A) MAS*H

B) HOGAN'S HEROES

C) THE WALTONS

D) LITTLE HOUSE ON THE PRAIRIE

26) WHAT WAS THE NAME OF THE FIRST SUCCESSFUL LIVER TRANSPLANT, PERFORMED IN 1963?

A) STARZL

B) MURRAY

C) BARNARD

D) DEBAKEY

27) WHICH ICONIC 1970S FILM STARRED ROBERT REDFORD AS A CON MAN WHO BECOMES A PRESIDENTIAL CANDIDATE?

A) THE CANDIDATE

B) THE STING

C) THE WAY WE WERE

D) THREE DAYS OF THE CONDOR

28) WHO WAS THE FAMOUS SINGER KNOWN AS THE "FIRST LADY OF ROCK" WHO ROSE TO FAME IN THE 1960S AND CONTINUED SUCCESS IN THE 1970S?

A) TINA TURNER

B) JANIS JOPLIN

C) CHER

D) ARETHA FRANKLIN

TIMELESS ✷ TRIVIA FOR ✷ SENIORS

Nostalgic Trivia

SENIORS TRIVIA EDITION

29) WHAT WAS THE NAME OF THE FIRST SUCCESSFUL HEART TRANSPLANT, PERFORMED IN 1967?

A) BARNARD
B) DEBAKEY
C) COOLEY
D) SHUMWAY

30) WHICH ICONIC 1970S FILM STARRED AL PACINO AS A NEW YORK CITY POLICE OFFICER?

A) SERPICO
B) THE GODFATHER
C) DOG DAY AFTERNOON
D) SCARFACE

31) WHO WAS THE FAMOUS SINGER KNOWN AS THE "KING OF FUNK" WHO ROSE TO FAME IN THE 1970S?

A) GEORGE CLINTON
B) JAMES BROWN
C) RICK JAMES
D) SLY STONE

32) WHICH ICONIC 1970S TV SHOW FEATURED A GROUP OF POLICE OFFICERS IN A FICTIONAL CITY IN CALIFORNIA?

A) STARSKY & HUTCH
B) HILL STREET BLUES
C) CHIPS
D) EMERGENCY!

TIMELESS ✳ TRIVIA FOR ✳ SENIORS

Nostalgic Trivia
Seniors Trivia Edition

33) WHICH ICONIC 1970S FILM STARRED JACK NICHOLSON AS A PRIVATE DETECTIVE IN LOS ANGELES?

A) CHINATOWN

B) ONE FLEW OVER THE CUCKOO'S NEST

C) THE SHINING

D) FIVE EASY PIECES

34) WHO WAS THE FAMOUS SINGER KNOWN AS THE "KING OF POP" WHO ROSE TO FAME AS A CHILD STAR IN THE 1960S AND CONTINUED SUCCESS IN THE 1970S?

A) MICHAEL JACKSON

B) PRINCE

C) STEVIE WONDER

D) MARVIN GAYE

35) WHICH ICONIC 1970S TV SHOW FEATURED A GROUP OF YOUNG PEOPLE LIVING IN A BEACH HOUSE IN CALIFORNIA?

A) THE BRADY BUNCH

B) CHARLIE'S ANGELS

C) THE PARTRIDGE FAMILY

D) THE MONKEES

36) WHAT WAS THE NAME OF THE FIRST SUCCESSFUL ARTIFICIAL HEART VALVE, DEVELOPED IN 1960?

A) STARR-EDWARDS

B) ST. JUDE MEDICAL

C) MEDTRONIC

D) EDWARDS LIFESCIENCES

TIMELESS ✶ TRIVIA FOR ✶ SENIORS

Nostalgic Trivia

37) WHO WAS THE FAMOUS SINGER KNOWN AS THE "QUEEN OF ROCK 'N' ROLL" WHO ROSE TO FAME IN THE 1970S?

A) TINA TURNER

B) STEVIE NICKS

C) PAT BENATAR

D) DEBBIE HARRY

38) WHICH ICONIC 1970S TV SHOW FEATURED A GROUP OF WOMEN WORKING AT A BREWERY IN BOSTON?

A) CHEERS

B) THE MARY TYLER MOORE SHOW

C) CHARLIE'S ANGELS

D) ALICE

39) WHAT WAS THE NAME OF THE FIRST SUCCESSFUL ARTIFICIAL HEART VALVE, DEVELOPED IN 1960?

A) STARR-EDWARDS

B) ST. JUDE MEDICAL

C) MEDTRONIC

D) EDWARDS LIFESCIENCES

40) WHICH ICONIC 1970S FILM STARRED GENE HACKMAN AS A SURVEILLANCE EXPERT WHO BECOMES PARANOID?

A) THE CONVERSATION

B) SERPICO

C) THE FRENCH CONNECTION

D) BULLITT

TIMELESS ✸ TRIVIA FOR ✸ SENIORS

41) WHICH ICONIC 1970S TV SHOW FEATURED A WEALTHY FAMILY IN DENVER WITH AN OIL BUSINESS?

A) DALLAS

B) DYNASTY

C) FALCON CREST

D) KNOTS LANDING

42) WHAT WAS THE NAME OF THE FIRST SUCCESSFUL HEART-LUNG TRANSPLANT, PERFORMED IN 1981?

A) SHUMWAY

B) COOPER

C) BARNARD

D) STARZL

43) WHICH ICONIC 1970S FILM STARRED JACK NICHOLSON AS A PATIENT IN A PSYCHIATRIC HOSPITAL?

A) ONE FLEW OVER THE CUCKOO'S NEST

B) CHINATOWN

C) THE SHINING

D) FIVE EASY PIECES

44) WHO WAS THE FAMOUS SINGER KNOWN AS THE "QUEEN OF DISCO" WHO ROSE TO FAME IN THE 1970S?

A) DONNA SUMMER

B) GLORIA GAYNOR

C) CHAKA KHAN

D) DIANA ROSS

SENIORS TRIVIA EDITION

Nostalgic Trivia

PAGENO. 38

---

45) WHAT WAS THE NAME OF THE FIRST SUCCESSFUL KIDNEY TRANSPLANT, PERFORMED IN 1954?

A) MURRAY

B) STARZL

C) BARNARD

D) HARDY

---

46) WHICH ICONIC 1970S FILM STARRED JOHN TRAVOLTA AS A BROOKLYN TEENAGER WHO BECOMES A DANCER?

A) SATURDAY NIGHT FEVER

B) GREASE

C) URBAN COWBOY

D) FOOTLOOSE

---

47) WHICH ICONIC 1970S TV SHOW FEATURED A GROUP OF AFRICAN AMERICAN FAMILIES LIVING IN A CHICAGO HOUSING PROJECT?

A) GOOD TIMES

B) SANFORD AND SON

C) THE JEFFERSONS

D) WHAT'S HAPPENING!!

---

48) WHICH ICONIC 1970S TV SHOW FEATURED A GROUP OF STUDENTS ATTENDING A HISTORICALLY BLACK COLLEGE?

A) THE JEFFERSONS

B) GOOD TIMES

C) SANFORD AND SON

D) A DIFFERENT WORLD

TIMELESS ✻ TRIVIA FOR ✻ SENIORS

Nostalgic Trivia

49) WHICH ICONIC 1970S FILM STARRED GENE WILDER AS A YOUNG FRANKENSTEIN HEIR?

A) YOUNG FRANKENSTEIN

B) BLAZING SADDLES

C) THE PRODUCERS

D) WILLY WONKA & THE CHOCOLATE FACTORY

50) WHO WAS THE FAMOUS SINGER KNOWN AS THE "HARDEST WORKING MAN IN SHOW BUSINESS" WHO ROSE TO FAME IN THE 1970S?

A) JAMES BROWN

B) BARRY WHITE

C) MARVIN GAYE

D) ISAAC HAYES

51) WHICH ICONIC 1970S MOVIE FEATURED THE SONG "STAYIN' ALIVE" BY THE BEE GEES?

A) SATURDAY NIGHT FEVER

B) GREASE

C) ROCKY

D) JAWS

52) WHAT WAS THE NAME OF THE FIRST SUCCESSFUL KIDNEY TRANSPLANT, PERFORMED IN 1954?

A) MURRAY

B) STARZL

C) BARNARD

D) HARDY

TIMELESS ✽ TRIVIA FOR ✽ SENIORS

4: Electrifying Eighties

1) WHICH ICONIC 1980S FILM STARRED TOM CRUISE AS A YOUNG RECRUIT AT A MILITARY ACADEMY?

A) TOP GUN
B) AN OFFICER AND A GENTLEMAN
C) PLATOON
D) FULL METAL JACKET

2) WHO WAS THE FAMOUS SINGER KNOWN AS THE "QUEEN OF POP" WHO ROSE TO FAME IN THE 1980S?

A) WHITNEY HOUSTON
B) MARIAH CAREY
C) MADONNA
D) CYNDI LAUPER

3) WHICH ICONIC 1980S TV SHOW FEATURED A GROUP OF FRIENDS LIVING IN BOSTON AND WORKING AT A BAR?

A) CHEERS
B) SEINFELD
C) FRIENDS
D) THE COSBY SHOW

4) WHAT WAS THE NAME OF THE FIRST SUCCESSFUL HEART-LUNG TRANSPLANT, PERFORMED IN 1981?

A) SHUMWAY
B) COOPER
C) BARNARD
D) STARZL

TIMELESS ✷ TRIVIA FOR ✷ SENIORS

SENIORS TRIVIA EDITION

Nostalgic Trivia

5) WHO WAS THE FAMOUS SINGER KNOWN AS THE "KING OF POP" WHO RELEASED HIT ALBUMS LIKE "THRILLER" IN THE 1980S?

A) MICHAEL JACKSON

B) PRINCE

C) MADONNA

D) WHITNEY HOUSTON

6) WHICH ICONIC 1980S TV SHOW FEATURED A GROUP OF FRIENDS ATTENDING A FICTIONAL COLLEGE IN BOSTON?

A) CHEERS

B) FAMILY TIES

C) THE COSBY SHOW

D) A DIFFERENT WORLD

7) WHAT WAS THE NAME OF THE FIRST SUCCESSFUL ARTIFICIAL HEART VALVE, DEVELOPED IN 1960?

A) STARR-EDWARDS

B) ST. JUDE MEDICAL

C) MEDTRONIC

D) EDWARDS LIFESCIENCES

8) WHICH ICONIC 1980S FILM STARRED MERYL STREEP AS A WOMAN WHO LEAVES HER FAMILY TO PURSUE HER SINGING DREAMS?

A) SILKWOOD

B) A CRY IN THE DARK

C) IRONWEED

D) POSTCARDS FROM THE EDGE

TIMELESS ✷ TRIVIA FOR ✷ SENIORS

SENIORS TRIVIA EDITION — Nostalgic Trivia — PAGE NO. 42

---

9) WHICH ICONIC 1980S TV SHOW FEATURED A GROUP OF FRIENDS LIVING IN NEW YORK CITY?

A) SEINFELD

B) FRIENDS

C) CHEERS

D) THE COSBY SHOW

---

10) WHAT WAS THE NAME OF THE FIRST SUCCESSFUL PANCREAS TRANSPLANT, PERFORMED IN 1966?

A) KELLY

B) LILLEHEI

C) STARZL

D) BARNARD

---

11) WHICH ICONIC 1980S FILM STARRED TOM CRUISE AS A YOUNG NAVY PILOT WHO FALLS IN LOVE WITH HIS INSTRUCTOR?

A) TOP GUN

B) AN OFFICER AND A GENTLEMAN

C) PLATOON

D) FULL METAL JACKET

---

12) WHO WAS THE FAMOUS SINGER KNOWN AS THE "QUEEN OF ROCK" WHO ROSE TO FAME IN THE 1970S AND CONTINUED HER SUCCESS IN THE 1980S?

A) TINA TURNER

B) STEVIE NICKS

C) PAT BENATAR

D) JOAN JETT

TIMELESS ✸ TRIVIA FOR ✸ SENIORS

SENIORS TRIVIA EDITION

Nostalgic Trivia

PAGE NO. 43

---

13) WHAT WAS THE NAME OF THE FIRST SUCCESSFUL ARTIFICIAL HEART IMPLANTED IN A HUMAN IN 1982?

A) JARVIK-7

B) ABIOCOR

C) SYNCARDIA

D) HEARTMATE

---

14) WHICH ICONIC 1980S FILM STARRED MOLLY RINGWALD AS A TEENAGER NAVIGATING THE COMPLEXITIES OF HIGH SCHOOL?

A) THE BREAKFAST CLUB

B) SIXTEEN CANDLES

C) PRETTY IN PINK

D) FERRIS BUELLER'S DAY OFF

---

15) WHO WAS THE FAMOUS SINGER KNOWN AS THE "QUEEN OF POP" WHO ROSE TO FAME IN THE 1990S?

A) WHITNEY HOUSTON

B) MARIAH CAREY

C) MADONNA

D) CYNDI LAUPER

---

16) WHICH ICONIC 1980S TV SHOW FEATURED A GROUP OF FRIENDS ATTENDING A HIGH SCHOOL IN WISCONSIN?

A) SAVED BY THE BELL

B) BEVERLY HILLS, 90210

C) THE WONDER YEARS

D) HAPPY DAYS

TIMELESS ✳ TRIVIA FOR ✳ SENIORS

SENIORS TRIVIA EDITION | **Nostalgic Trivia** | **PAGE NO. 44**

---

17) WHICH ICONIC 1980S FILM STARRED PATRICK SWAYZE AS A BOUNCER WHO BECOMES INVOLVED IN THE UNDERGROUND WORLD OF BAR FIGHTS?

A) ROADHOUSE

B) DIRTY DANCING

C) GHOST

D) POINT BREAK

---

18) WHO WAS THE FAMOUS SINGER KNOWN AS THE "QUEEN OF SOUL" WHO CONTINUED HER SUCCESS IN THE 1980S?

A) ARETHA FRANKLIN

B) TINA TURNER

C) DIANA ROSS

D) WHITNEY HOUSTON

---

19) WHICH ICONIC 1980S TV SHOW FEATURED A GROUP OF FRIENDS LIVING IN NEW YORK CITY AND EXPLORING VARIOUS DATING SCENARIOS?

A) SEINFELD

B) FRIENDS

C) CHEERS

D) THE COSBY SHOW

---

20) WHAT WAS THE NAME OF THE FIRST SUCCESSFUL LIVER TRANSPLANT, PERFORMED IN 1963?

A) STARZL

B) MURRAY

C) BARNARD

D) DEBAKEY

TIMELESS ✷ TRIVIA FOR ✷ SENIORS

Nostalgic Trivia

SENIORS TRIVIA EDITION

21) WHO WAS THE FAMOUS SINGER KNOWN AS THE "MATERIAL GIRL" WHO ROSE TO FAME IN THE 1980S?

A) CYNDI LAUPER

B) TINA TURNER

C) MADONNA

D) WHITNEY HOUSTON

22) WHICH ICONIC 1980S TV SHOW FEATURED A GROUP OF FRIENDS LIVING IN BOSTON?

A) CHEERS

B) SEINFELD

C) FRIENDS

D) THE COSBY SHOW

23) WHAT WAS THE NAME OF THE FIRST SUCCESSFUL HEART TRANSPLANT, PERFORMED IN 1967?

A) BARNARD

B) DEBAKEY

C) COOLEY

D) SHUMWAY

24) WHICH ICONIC 1980S FILM STARRED TOM HANKS AS A YOUNG MAN WHO FINDS HIMSELF WORKING AT A LARGE CORPORATION?

A) BIG

B) WORKING GIRL

C) 9 TO 5

D) BABY BOOM

TIMELESS ✻ TRIVIA FOR ✻ SENIORS

Nostalgic Trivia

SENIORS TRIVIA EDITION

25) WHICH ICONIC 1980S TV SHOW FEATURED A GROUP OF FOUR SINGLE WOMEN LIVING IN MIAMI?

A) THE GOLDEN GIRLS

B) DESIGNING WOMEN

C) CAGNEY & LACEY

D) MURPHY BROWN

26) WHAT WAS THE NAME OF THE FIRST SUCCESSFUL LUNG TRANSPLANT, PERFORMED IN 1963?

A) HARDY

B) COOPER

C) BARNARD

D) STARZL

27) WHICH ICONIC 1980S FILM STARRED DUSTIN HOFFMAN AS AN ACTOR WHO TAKES ON THE ROLE OF A WOMAN TO LAND A JOB?

A) TOOTSIE

B) MRS. DOUBTFIRE

C) YENTL

D) VICTOR/VICTORIA

28) WHO WAS THE FAMOUS SINGER KNOWN AS THE "QUEEN OF SOUL" WHO ROSE TO FAME IN THE 1960S AND CONTINUED HER SUCCESS IN THE 1980S?

A) ARETHA FRANKLIN

B) TINA TURNER

C) DIANA ROSS

D) WHITNEY HOUSTON

TIMELESS ✻ TRIVIA FOR ✻ SENIORS

Nostalgic Trivia

29) WHAT WAS THE NAME OF THE FIRST SUCCESSFUL HEART-LUNG TRANSPLANT, PERFORMED IN 1981?

A) SHUMWAY

B) COOPER

C) BARNARD

D) STARZL

30) WHICH ICONIC 1980S FILM STARRED TOM HANKS AS A YOUNG MAN WHO BECOMES A MERMAID'S OBJECT OF AFFECTION?

A) SPLASH

B) THE LITTLE MERMAID

C) PRETTY WOMAN

D) ENCHANTED

31) WHO WAS THE FAMOUS SINGER KNOWN AS THE "QUEEN OF SOUL" WHO ROSE TO FAME IN THE 1960S AND CONTINUED HER SUCCESS IN THE 1980S?

A) ARETHA FRANKLIN

B) TINA TURNER

C) DIANA ROSS

D) WHITNEY HOUSTON

32) WHICH ICONIC 1980S TV SHOW FEATURED A GROUP OF FRIENDS ATTENDING A HIGH SCHOOL IN PHILADELPHIA?

A) SAVED BY THE BELL

B) BEVERLY HILLS, 90210

C) THE WONDER YEARS

D) THE FRESH PRINCE OF BEL-AIR

TIMELESS ✸ TRIVIA FOR ✸ SENIORS

SENIORS TRIVIA EDITION

Nostalgic Trivia

33) WHICH ICONIC 1980S FILM STARRED MEL GIBSON AS A POLICE OFFICER IN A FUTURISTIC LOS ANGELES?

A) LETHAL WEAPON
B) MAD MAX
C) ROBOCOP
D) BLADE RUNNER

34) WHO WAS THE FAMOUS SINGER KNOWN AS THE "QUEEN OF POP ROCK" WHO ROSE TO FAME IN THE 1980S?

A) PAT BENATAR
B) STEVIE NICKS
C) DEBBIE HARRY
D) JOAN JETT

35) WHICH ICONIC 1980S TV SHOW FEATURED A GROUP OF FRIENDS ATTENDING A HIGH SCHOOL IN CALIFORNIA?

A) SAVED BY THE BELL
B) BEVERLY HILLS, 90210
C) THE WONDER YEARS
D) FREAKS AND GEEKS

36) WHAT WAS THE NAME OF THE FIRST SUCCESSFUL PANCREAS TRANSPLANT, PERFORMED IN 1966?

A) KELLY
B) LILLEHEI
C) STARZL
D) BARNARD

TIMELESS ✳ TRIVIA FOR ✳ SENIORS

37) WHO WAS THE FAMOUS SINGER KNOWN AS THE "PURPLE RAIN" ARTIST WHO ROSE TO FAME IN THE 1980S?

A) MICHAEL JACKSON

B) PRINCE

C) GEORGE MICHAEL

D) LIONEL RICHIE

---

38) WHICH ICONIC 1980S TV SHOW FEATURED A GROUP OF OLDER WOMEN LIVING IN MIAMI?

A) THE GOLDEN GIRLS

B) DESIGNING WOMEN

C) CAGNEY & LACEY

D) MURPHY BROWN

---

39) WHAT WAS THE NAME OF THE FIRST SUCCESSFUL ARTIFICIAL HEART IMPLANTED IN A HUMAN IN 1982?

A) JARVIK-7

B) ABIOCOR

C) SYNCARDIA

D) HEARTMATE

---

40) WHICH ICONIC 1980S FILM STARRED TOM CRUISE AS A YOUNG MAN WHO TAKES A JOB AS A TRAFFIC REPORTER?

A) TOP GUN

B) COCKTAIL

C) RISKY BUSINESS

D) THE FIRM

TIMELESS ✷ TRIVIA FOR ✷ SENIORS

Nostalgic Trivia

SENIORS TRIVIA EDITION

PAGE NO. 50

---

41) WHICH ICONIC 1980S TV SHOW FEATURED A GROUP OF TEENAGERS ATTENDING A HIGH SCHOOL IN INDIANA?

A) SAVED BY THE BELL

B) BEVERLY HILLS, 90210

C) THE WONDER YEARS

D) FREAKS AND GEEKS

---

42) WHAT WAS THE NAME OF THE FIRST SUCCESSFUL KIDNEY TRANSPLANT, PERFORMED IN 1954?

A) MURRAY

B) STARZL

C) BARNARD

D) HARDY

---

43) WHICH ICONIC 1980S FILM STARRED MICHAEL J. FOX AS A TEENAGER WHO TRAVELS THROUGH TIME IN A DELOREAN?

A) BACK TO THE FUTURE

B) FERRIS BUELLER'S DAY OFF

C) SIXTEEN CANDLES

D) THE BREAKFAST CLUB

---

44) WHO WAS THE FAMOUS SINGER KNOWN AS THE "QUEEN OF POP" WHO ROSE TO FAME IN THE 1980S?

A) WHITNEY HOUSTON

B) MARIAH CAREY

C) MADONNA

D) CYNDI LAUPER

TIMELESS ✶ TRIVIA FOR ✶ SENIORS

45) WHAT WAS THE NAME OF THE FIRST SUCCESSFUL LIVER TRANSPLANT, PERFORMED IN 1963?

A) STARZL

B) MURRAY

C) BARNARD

D) DEBAKEY

46) WHICH ICONIC 1980S FILM STARRED KEVIN BACON AS A TEENAGER WHO TRIES TO SPREAD A DANCE CRAZE ACROSS THE NATION?

A) FOOTLOOSE

B) DIRTY DANCING

C) FLASHDANCE

D) BREAKIN'

47) WHICH ICONIC 1980S TV SHOW FEATURED A GROUP OF FRIENDS ATTENDING A SCHOOL IN NEW YORK CITY?

A) SAVED BY THE BELL

B) BEVERLY HILLS, 90210

C) THE WONDER YEARS

D) FAME

48) WHICH ICONIC 1980S TV SHOW FEATURED A GROUP OF FRIENDS ATTENDING A HIGH SCHOOL IN CALIFORNIA?

A) SAVED BY THE BELL

B) BEVERLY HILLS, 90210

C) THE WONDER YEARS

D) FREAKS AND GEEKS

Nostalgic Trivia

SENIORS TRIVIA EDITION

PAGE NO. 52

---

49) WHICH ICONIC 1980S FILM STARRED ARNOLD SCHWARZENEGGER AS A CYBORG SENT FROM THE FUTURE TO PROTECT A YOUNG BOY?

- A) THE TERMINATOR
- B) PREDATOR
- C) TOTAL RECALL
- D) COMMANDO

---

50) WHO WAS THE FAMOUS SINGER KNOWN AS THE "QUEEN OF SOUL" WHO ROSE TO FAME IN THE 1960S AND CONTINUED HER SUCCESS IN THE 1980S?

- A) ARETHA FRANKLIN
- B) TINA TURNER
- C) DIANA ROSS
- D) WHITNEY HOUSTON

---

51) WHICH 1980S TELEVISION SERIES FEATURED THE CHARACTER J.R. EWING, KNOWN FOR HIS DEVIOUS BUSINESS DEALINGS?

- A) MIAMI VICE
- B) MAGNUM, P.I.
- C) DALLAS
- D) THE A-TEAM

---

52) WHAT WAS THE NAME OF THE FIRST SUCCESSFUL LUNG TRANSPLANT, PERFORMED IN 1963?

- A) HARDY
- B) COOPER
- C) BARNARD
- D) STARZL

TIMELESS ✳ TRIVIA FOR ✳ SENIORS

| SENIORS TRIVIA EDITION | # 5: Gnarly Nineties | PAGE NO. 53 |

1) WHICH ICONIC 1990S TV SHOW FEATURED A GROUP OF FRIENDS LIVING IN NEW YORK CITY?

- A) SEINFELD
- B) FRIENDS
- C) FRASIER
- D) THE FRESH PRINCE OF BEL-AIR

2) WHO WAS THE FAMOUS SINGER KNOWN AS THE "QUEEN OF POP" WHO ROSE TO FAME IN THE 1980S AND CONTINUED HER SUCCESS IN THE 1990S?

- A) WHITNEY HOUSTON
- B) MARIAH CAREY
- C) MADONNA
- D) CYNDI LAUPER

3) WHICH ICONIC 1990S FILM STARRED WHOOPI GOLDBERG AS A PSYCHIC WHO HELPS A MAN RECONNECT WITH HIS DECEASED WIFE?

- A) GHOST
- B) THE SIXTH SENSE
- C) GHOSTBUSTERS
- D) WHAT DREAMS MAY COME

4) WHAT WAS THE NAME OF THE FIRST SUCCESSFUL LIVER TRANSPLANT, PERFORMED IN 1963?

- A) STARZL
- B) MURRAY
- C) BARNARD
- D) DEBAKEY

TIMELESS ✳ TRIVIA FOR ✳ SENIORS

| SENIORS TRIVIA EDITION | Nostalgic Trivia | PAGENO. 54 |

5) WHO WAS THE FAMOUS SINGER KNOWN AS THE "QUEEN OF POP" WHO ROSE TO FAME IN THE 1990S WITH HITS LIKE "VISION OF LOVE"?

A) WHITNEY HOUSTON

B) MARIAH CAREY

C) CHRISTINA AGUILERA

D) BRITNEY SPEARS

6) WHICH ICONIC 1990S FILM STARRED MEG RYAN AS A WOMAN WHO FALLS IN LOVE WITH A MAN SHE ONLY KNOWS THROUGH EMAILS?

A) YOU'VE GOT MAIL

B) SLEEPLESS IN SEATTLE

C) WHEN HARRY MET SALLY

D) FRENCH KISS

7) WHAT WAS THE NAME OF THE FIRST SUCCESSFUL PANCREAS TRANSPLANT, PERFORMED IN 1966?

A) KELLY

B) LILLEHEI

C) STARZL

D) BARNARD

8) WHICH ICONIC 1990S TV SHOW FEATURED A GROUP OF FRIENDS LIVING IN NEW YORK CITY AND EXPLORING DIFFERENT ROMANTIC RELATIONSHIPS?

A) SEINFELD

B) FRIENDS

C) FRASIER

D) SEX AND THE CITY

TIMELESS ✳ TRIVIA FOR ✳ SENIORS

9) WHICH ICONIC 1990S FILM STARRED TOM HANKS AS A MAN STRANDED ON A DESERTED ISLAND?

A) CAST AWAY

B) FORREST GUMP

C) SAVING PRIVATE RYAN

D) THE GREEN MILE

10) WHAT WAS THE NAME OF THE FIRST SUCCESSFUL LIVER TRANSPLANT, PERFORMED IN 1963?

A) STARZL

B) MURRAY

C) BARNARD

D) DEBAKEY

11) WHICH ICONIC 1990S TV SHOW FEATURED A GROUP OF FRIENDS LIVING IN NEW YORK CITY AND EXPLORING DIFFERENT ROMANTIC RELATIONSHIPS?

A) SEINFELD

B) FRIENDS

C) FRASIER

D) SEX AND THE CITY

12) WHO WAS THE FAMOUS SINGER KNOWN AS THE "QUEEN OF HIP-HOP SOUL" WHO ROSE TO FAME IN THE 1990S WITH HITS LIKE "YOU'RE ALL I NEED TO GET BY"?

A) LAURYN HILL

B) MARY J. BLIGE

C) ERYKAH BADU

D) MISSY ELLIOTT

TIMELESS ✶ TRIVIA FOR ✶ SENIORS

Nostalgic Trivia

SENIORS TRIVIA EDITION

13) WHAT WAS THE NAME OF THE FIRST SUCCESSFUL ARTIFICIAL HEART VALVE, DEVELOPED IN 1960?

A) STARR-EDWARDS

B) ST. JUDE MEDICAL

C) MEDTRONIC

D) EDWARDS LIFESCIENCES

14) WHICH ICONIC 1990S TV SHOW FEATURED A GROUP OF TEENAGERS ATTENDING A HIGH SCHOOL IN BEVERLY HILLS, CALIFORNIA?

A) SAVED BY THE BELL

B) BEVERLY HILLS, 90210

C) THE WONDER YEARS

D) FREAKS AND GEEKS

15) WHO WAS THE FAMOUS SINGER KNOWN AS THE "QUEEN OF R&B" WHO ROSE TO FAME IN THE 1990S WITH HITS LIKE "EXHALE (SHOOP SHOOP)"?

A) AALIYAH

B) TLC

C) BRANDY

D) WHITNEY HOUSTON

16) WHICH ICONIC 1990S FILM STARRED KEANU REEVES AS A COMPUTER HACKER WHO DISCOVERS A SHOCKING TRUTH ABOUT THE WORLD?

A) THE MATRIX

B) SPEED

C) POINT BREAK

D) JOHNNY MNEMONIC

TIMELESS ✳ TRIVIA FOR ✳ SENIORS

Nostalgic Trivia

SENIORS TRIVIA EDITION

17) WHICH ICONIC 1990S TV SHOW FEATURED A GROUP OF TEENAGERS ATTENDING A HIGH SCHOOL IN CALIFORNIA?

  A) SAVED BY THE BELL
  B) BEVERLY HILLS, 90210
  C) THE WONDER YEARS
  D) FREAKS AND GEEKS

18) WHO WAS THE FAMOUS SINGER KNOWN AS THE "QUEEN OF HIP-HOP SOUL" WHO ROSE TO FAME IN THE 1990S WITH HITS LIKE "DOO WOP (THAT THING)"?

  A) LAURYN HILL
  B) MARY J. BLIGE
  C) ERYKAH BADU
  D) MISSY ELLIOTT

19) WHICH ICONIC 1990S FILM STARRED ROBIN WILLIAMS AS A TEACHER WHO INSPIRES HIS STUDENTS THROUGH UNORTHODOX METHODS?

  A) DEAD POETS SOCIETY
  B) PATCH ADAMS
  C) GOOD WILL HUNTING
  D) MRS. DOUBTFIRE

20) WHAT WAS THE NAME OF THE FIRST SUCCESSFUL HEART TRANSPLANT, PERFORMED IN 1967?

  A) BARNARD
  B) DEBAKEY
  C) COOLEY
  D) SHUMWAY

TIMELESS * TRIVIA FOR * SENIORS

| SENIORS TRIVIA EDITION | Nostalgic Trivia | PAGE NO. 58 |

21) WHO WAS THE FAMOUS SINGER KNOWN AS THE "PRINCESS OF POP" WHO ROSE TO FAME IN THE 1990S WITH HITS LIKE "...BABY ONE MORE TIME"?

A) CHRISTINA AGUILERA

B) BRITNEY SPEARS

C) JESSICA SIMPSON

D) MANDY MOORE

22) WHICH ICONIC 1990S FILM STARRED MEL GIBSON AS A MAN WHO TRAVELS THROUGH TIME TO TRY AND PREVENT A TRAGEDY?

A) RANSOM

B) BRAVEHEART

C) LETHAL WEAPON 4

D) THE PATRIOT

23) WHAT WAS THE NAME OF THE FIRST SUCCESSFUL LUNG TRANSPLANT, PERFORMED IN 1963?

A) HARDY

B) COOPER

C) BARNARD

D) STARZL

24) WHICH ICONIC 1990S TV SHOW FEATURED A GROUP OF FRIENDS LIVING IN NEW YORK CITY AND EXPLORING DIFFERENT ROMANTIC RELATIONSHIPS?

A) SEINFELD

B) FRIENDS

C) FRASIER

D) SEX AND THE CITY

TIMELESS ✷ TRIVIA FOR ✷ SENIORS

SENIORS TRIVIA EDITION — Nostalgic Trivia

25) WHICH ICONIC 1990S FILM STARRED JULIA ROBERTS AS A VIVACIOUS WOMAN WHO CHARMS A WEALTHY BUSINESSMAN?

- A) PRETTY WOMAN
- B) RUNAWAY BRIDE
- C) NOTTING HILL
- D) MY BEST FRIEND'S WEDDING

26) WHAT WAS THE NAME OF THE FIRST SUCCESSFUL ARTIFICIAL HEART IMPLANTED IN A HUMAN IN 1982?

- A) JARVIK-7
- B) ABIOCOR
- C) SYNCARDIA
- D) HEARTMATE

27) WHICH ICONIC 1990S TV SHOW FEATURED A GROUP OF FRIENDS LIVING IN SEATTLE AND WORKING AT A COFFEE SHOP?

- A) SEINFELD
- B) FRIENDS
- C) FRASIER
- D) FELICITY

28) WHO WAS THE FAMOUS SINGER KNOWN AS THE "QUEEN OF R&B" WHO ROSE TO FAME IN THE 1990S WITH HITS LIKE "THE BOY IS MINE"?

- A) AALIYAH
- B) TLC
- C) BRANDY
- D) MONICA

TIMELESS * TRIVIA FOR * SENIORS

29) WHAT WAS THE NAME OF THE FIRST SUCCESSFUL KIDNEY TRANSPLANT, PERFORMED IN 1954?

A) MURRAY
B) STARZL
C) BARNARD
D) HARDY

30) WHICH ICONIC 1990S TV SHOW FEATURED A GROUP OF FRIENDS LIVING IN NEW YORK CITY AND A COFFEE SHOP AS A CENTRAL HANGOUT?

A) SEINFELD
B) FRIENDS
C) FRASIER
D) WILL & GRACE

31) WHO WAS THE FAMOUS SINGER KNOWN AS THE "QUEEN OF HIP-HOP SOUL" WHO ROSE TO FAME IN THE 1990S WITH HITS LIKE "NO DIGGITY"?

A) LAURYN HILL
B) MARY J. BLIGE
C) ERYKAH BADU
D) BLACKSTREET

32) WHICH ICONIC 1990S FILM STARRED BEN AFFLECK AND MATT DAMON AS YOUNG MATH GENIUSES?

A) GOOD WILL HUNTING
B) CHASING AMY
C) DOGMA
D) CLERKS

SENIORS TRIVIA EDITION — **Nostalgic Trivia** — PAGE NO. 61

---

33) WHICH ICONIC 1990S TV SHOW FEATURED A GROUP OF FRIENDS LIVING IN BOSTON AND WORKING AT A BAR?

A) CHEERS
B) FRASIER
C) FRIENDS
D) WILL & GRACE

---

34) WHO WAS THE FAMOUS SINGER KNOWN AS THE "QUEEN OF POP ROCK" WHO ROSE TO FAME IN THE 1980S AND CONTINUED HER SUCCESS IN THE 1990S?

A) PAT BENATAR
B) STEVIE NICKS
C) DEBBIE HARRY
D) JOAN JETT

---

35) WHICH ICONIC 1990S FILM STARRED BRAD PITT AND EDWARD NORTON AS MEMBERS OF AN UNDERGROUND FIGHT CLUB?

A) FIGHT CLUB
B) SEVEN
C) THE SIXTH SENSE
D) AMERICAN BEAUTY

---

36) WHAT WAS THE NAME OF THE FIRST SUCCESSFUL KIDNEY TRANSPLANT, PERFORMED IN 1954?

A) MURRAY
B) STARZL
C) BARNARD
D) HARDY

TIMELESS ✳ TRIVIA FOR ✳ SENIORS

Nostalgic Trivia

37) WHO WAS THE FAMOUS SINGER KNOWN AS THE "QUEEN OF R&B" WHO ROSE TO FAME IN THE 1990S WITH HITS LIKE "WATERFALLS"?

A) AALIYAH
B) TLC
C) BRANDY
D) MONICA

38) WHICH ICONIC 1990S FILM STARRED TOM HANKS AS A SOLDIER WHO IS PART OF THE N ORMANDY INVASION DURING WORLD WAR II?

A) FORREST GUMP
B) CAST AWAY
C) SAVING PRIVATE RYAN
D) THE GREEN MILE

39) WHAT WAS THE NAME OF THE FIRST SUCCESSFUL ARTIFICIAL HEART VALVE, DEVELOPED IN 1960?

A) STARR-EDWARDS
B) ST. JUDE MEDICAL
C) MEDTRONIC
D) EDWARDS LIFESCIENCES

40) WHICH ICONIC 1990S TV SHOW FEATURED A GROUP OF FRIENDS LIVING IN NEW YORK CITY AND EXPLORING DIFFERENT ROMANTIC RELATIONSHIPS?

A) SEINFELD
B) FRIENDS
C) FRASIER
D) SEX AND THE CITY

TIMELESS ✶ TRIVIA FOR ✶ SENIORS

SENIORS TRIVIA EDITION

Nostalgic Trivia

PAGE NO. 63

---

41) WHICH ICONIC 1990S FILM STARRED TOM HANKS AS A SLOW-WITTED BUT KIND-HEARTED MAN WHO WITNESSES HISTORICAL EVENTS?

A) FORREST GUMP

B) CAST AWAY

C) SAVING PRIVATE RYAN

D) THE GREEN MILE

---

42) WHAT WAS THE NAME OF THE FIRST SUCCESSFUL HEART-LUNG TRANSPLANT, PERFORMED IN 1981?

A) SHUMWAY

B) COOPER

C) BARNARD

D) STARZL

---

43) WHICH ICONIC 1990S TV SHOW FEATURED A GROUP OF WOMEN LIVING IN MIAMI, FLORIDA?

A) THE GOLDEN GIRLS

B) CYBILL

C) GRACE UNDER FIRE

D) THE NANNY

---

44) WHO WAS THE FAMOUS SINGER KNOWN AS THE "QUEEN OF POP" WHO ROSE TO FAME IN THE 1990S WITH HITS LIKE "OOPS!...I DID IT AGAIN"?

A) CHRISTINA AGUILERA

B) BRITNEY SPEARS

C) JESSICA SIMPSON

D) MANDY MOORE

TIMELESS ✱ TRIVIA FOR ✱ SENIORS

Nostalgic Trivia

45) WHAT WAS THE NAME OF THE FIRST SUCCESSFUL HEART TRANSPLANT, PERFORMED IN 1967?

A) BARNARD

B) DEBAKEY

C) COOLEY

D) SHUMWAY

46) WHICH ICONIC 1990S TV SHOW FEATURED A GROUP OF FRIENDS LIVING IN NEW YORK CITY AND EXPLORING VARIOUS DATING SCENARIOS?

A) SEINFELD

B) FRIENDS

C) FRASIER

D) SEX AND THE CITY

47) WHO WAS THE FAMOUS SINGER KNOWN AS THE "QUEEN OF POP" WHO ROSE TO FAME IN THE 1980S AND CONTINUED HER SUCCESS IN THE 1990S?

A) WHITNEY HOUSTON

B) MARIAH CAREY

C) MADONNA

D) CYNDI LAUPER

48) WHICH ICONIC 1990S FILM STARRED LEONARDO DICAPRIO AND KATE WINSLET AS PASSENGERS ON THE ILL-FATED TITANIC?

A) TITANIC

B) PEARL HARBOR

C) THE PATRIOT

D) ARMAGEDDON

TIMELESS * TRIVIA FOR * SENIORS

Nostalgic Trivia

SENIORS TRIVIA EDITION

49) WHICH ICONIC 1990S TV SHOW FEATURED A GROUP OF FRIENDS LIVING IN NEW YORK CITY AND A COFFEE SHOP AS A CENTRAL HANGOUT?

A) SEINFELD
B) FRIENDS
C) FRASIER
D) WILL & GRACE

50) WHO WAS THE FAMOUS SINGER KNOWN AS THE "QUEEN OF HIP-HOP" WHO ROSE TO FAME IN THE 1990S WITH HITS LIKE "DOO WOP (THAT THING)"?

A) LAURYN HILL
B) MARY J. BLIGE
C) ERYKAH BADU
D) MISSY ELLIOTT

51) WHICH ICONIC 1990S FILM STARRED TOM HANKS AS A PRISON GUARD DURING THE GREAT DEPRESSION?

A) THE GREEN MILE
B) FORREST GUMP
C) CAST AWAY
D) SAVING PRIVATE RYAN

52) WHAT WAS THE NAME OF THE FIRST SUCCESSFUL PANCREAS TRANSPLANT, PERFORMED IN 1966?

A) KELLY
B) LILLEHEI
C) STARZL
D) BARNARD

TIMELESS ✻ TRIVIA FOR ✻ SENIORS

SENIORS TRIVIA EDITION

6: Millennial Memories

1) WHICH ICONIC EARLY 2000S TV SHOW FEATURED A GROUP OF FRIENDS LIVING IN NEW YORK CITY?

    A) FRIENDS

    B) HOW I MET YOUR MOTHER

    C) THE BIG BANG THEORY

    D) GOSSIP GIRL

2) WHO WAS THE FAMOUS SINGER KNOWN AS THE "QUEEN OF R&B" WHO ROSE TO FAME IN THE LATE 1990S AND CONTINUED HER SUCCESS IN THE EARLY 2000S?

    A) AALIYAH

    B) BEYONCÃ Â Ã Â©

    C) ALICIA KEYS

    D) RIHANNA

3) WHICH ICONIC EARLY 2000S FILM STARRED DANIEL RADCLIFFE AS A YOUNG WIZARD ATTENDING THE HOGWARTS SCHOOL OF WITCHCRAFT AND WIZARDRY?

    A) HARRY POTTER AND THE SORCERER'S STONE

    B) HARRY POTTER AND THE CHAMBER OF SECRETS

    C) HARRY POTTER AND THE PRISONER OF AZKABAN

    D) HARRY POTTER AND THE GOBLET OF FIRE

4) WHAT WAS THE NAME OF THE FIRST SUCCESSFUL HEART-LUNG TRANSPLANT, PERFORMED IN 1981?

    A) SHUMWAY

    B) COOPER

    C) BARNARD

    D) STARZL

TIMELESS ✱ TRIVIA FOR ✱ SENIORS

Nostalgic Trivia

SENIORS TRIVIA EDITION

5) WHO WAS THE FAMOUS SINGER KNOWN AS THE "PRINCESS OF POP" WHO ROSE TO FAME IN THE LATE 1990S AND CONTINUED HER SUCCESS IN THE EARLY 2000S?

A) CHRISTINA AGUILERA
B) BRITNEY SPEARS
C) JESSICA SIMPSON
D) MANDY MOORE

6) WHICH ICONIC EARLY 2000S FILM STARRED KEANU REEVES AS A SKILLED HACKER WHO TRIES TO PREVENT A WORLDWIDE COMPUTER CRASH?

A) THE MATRIX RELOADED
B) THE MATRIX REVOLUTIONS
C) THE MATRIX
D) JOHNNY MNEMONIC

7) WHAT WAS THE NAME OF THE FIRST SUCCESSFUL PANCREAS TRANSPLANT, PERFORMED IN 1966?

A) KELLY
B) LILLEHEI
C) STARZL
D) BARNARD

8) WHICH ICONIC EARLY 2000S TV SHOW FEATURED A GROUP OF FRIENDS LIVING IN NEW YORK CITY AND EXPLORING DIFFERENT ROMANTIC RELATIONSHIPS?

A) FRIENDS
B) HOW I MET YOUR MOTHER
C) THE BIG BANG THEORY
D) SEX AND THE CITY

TIMELESS ✱ TRIVIA FOR ✱ SENIORS

| SENIORS TRIVIA EDITION | **Nostalgic Trivia** | PAGE NO. 68 |

9) WHICH ICONIC EARLY 2000S FILM STARRED TOBEY MAGUIRE AS A HIGH SCHOOL STUDENT WHO GAINS SUPERPOWERS?

A) SPIDER-MAN
B) X-MEN
C) IRON MAN
D) THE HULK

10) WHAT WAS THE NAME OF THE FIRST SUCCESSFUL KIDNEY TRANSPLANT, PERFORMED IN 1954?

A) MURRAY
B) STARZL
C) BARNARD
D) HARDY

11) WHICH ICONIC EARLY 2000S TV SHOW FEATURED A GROUP OF FRIENDS LIVING IN LOS ANGELES AND EXPLORING DIFFERENT ROMANTIC RELATIONSHIPS?

A) FRIENDS
B) HOW I MET YOUR MOTHER
C) THE BIG BANG THEORY
D) THE O.C.

12) WHO WAS THE FAMOUS SINGER KNOWN AS THE "QUEEN OF R&B" WHO ROSE TO FAME IN THE LATE 1990S AND CONTINUED HER SUCCESS IN THE EARLY 2000S?

A) AALIYAH
B) BEYONCÃ Â Ã Â©
C) ALICIA KEYS
D) RIHANNA

TIMELESS ✱ TRIVIA FOR ✱ SENIORS

Nostalgic Trivia

SENIORS TRIVIA EDITION

13) WHAT WAS THE NAME OF THE FIRST SUCCESSFUL ARTIFICIAL HEART VALVE, DEVELOPED IN 1960?

A) STARR-EDWARDS

B) ST. JUDE MEDICAL

C) MEDTRONIC

D) EDWARDS LIFESCIENCES

14) WHICH ICONIC EARLY 2000S TV SHOW FEATURED A GROUP OF FRIENDS LIVING IN NEW YORK CITY AND WORKING AT A COFFEE SHOP?

A) FRIENDS

B) HOW I MET YOUR MOTHER

C) THE BIG BANG THEORY

D) GOSSIP GIRL

15) WHO WAS THE FAMOUS SINGER KNOWN AS THE "QUEEN OF POP" WHO ROSE TO FAME IN THE LATE 1990S AND CONTINUED HER SUCCESS IN THE EARLY 2000S?

A) CHRISTINA AGUILERA

B) BRITNEY SPEARS

C) JESSICA SIMPSON

D) MANDY MOORE

16) WHICH ICONIC EARLY 2000S FILM STARRED HEATH LEDGER AND JAKE GYLLENHAAL AS COWBOYS IN LOVE?

A) BROKEBACK MOUNTAIN

B) JARHEAD

C) THE PATRIOT

D) BLACK HAWK DOWN

TIMELESS ✳ TRIVIA FOR ✳ SENIORS

| SENIORS TRIVIA EDITION | **Nostalgic Trivia** | PAGENO. 70 |

17) WHICH ICONIC EARLY 2000S TV SHOW FEATURED A GROUP OF TEENAGERS ATTENDING A HIGH SCHOOL IN CALIFORNIA?

A) THE O.C.
B) ONE TREE HILL
C) DAWSON'S CREEK
D) GILMORE GIRLS

18) WHO WAS THE FAMOUS SINGER KNOWN AS THE "QUEEN OF NEO-SOUL" WHO ROSE TO FAME IN THE EARLY 2000S WITH HITS LIKE "FALLIN'"?

A) AALIYAH
B) BEYONCÃ Â Ã Â©
C) ALICIA KEYS
D) RIHANNA

19) WHICH ICONIC EARLY 2000S FILM STARRED RUSSELL CROWE AS A BRILLIANT MATHEMATICIAN WHO BECOMES A CODE-BREAKER FOR THE GOVERNMENT?

A) A BEAUTIFUL MIND
B) THE INSIDER
C) GLADIATOR
D) MASTER AND COMMANDER: THE FAR SIDE OF THE WORLD

20) WHAT WAS THE NAME OF THE FIRST SUCCESSFUL LIVER TRANSPLANT, PERFORMED IN 1963?

A) STARZL
B) MURRAY
C) BARNARD
D) DEBAKEY

TIMELESS ✶ TRIVIA FOR ✶ SENIORS

Nostalgic Trivia

SENIORS TRIVIA EDITION

21) WHO WAS THE FAMOUS SINGER KNOWN AS THE "QUEEN OF POP" WHO ROSE TO FAME IN THE 1980S AND CONTINUED HER SUCCESS IN THE EARLY 2000S?

A) WHITNEY HOUSTON
B) MARIAH CAREY
C) MADONNA
D) BRITNEY SPEARS

22) WHICH ICONIC EARLY 2000S FILM STARRED VIN DIESEL AS A STREET RACER WHO GETS CAUGHT UP IN A HIGH-STAKES HEIST?

A) THE FAST AND THE FURIOUS
B) 2 FAST 2 FURIOUS
C) THE ITALIAN JOB
D) GONE IN 60 SECONDS

23) WHAT WAS THE NAME OF THE FIRST SUCCESSFUL LUNG TRANSPLANT, PERFORMED IN 1963?

A) HARDY
B) COOPER
C) BARNARD
D) STARZL

24) WHICH ICONIC EARLY 2000S TV SHOW FEATURED A GROUP OF FRIENDS LIVING IN NEW YORK CITY AND EXPLORING DIFFERENT ROMANTIC RELATIONSHIPS?

A) FRIENDS
B) HOW I MET YOUR MOTHER
C) THE BIG BANG THEORY
D) SEX AND THE CITY

TIMELESS ✷ TRIVIA FOR ✷ SENIORS

SENIORS TRIVIA EDITION — Nostalgic Trivia — PAGENO. 72

25) WHICH ICONIC EARLY 2000S FILM STARRED WILL SMITH AS A TALENTED BOXER WHO BECOMES A HEAVYWEIGHT CHAMPION?

A) ALI

B) THE PURSUIT OF HAPPYNESS

C) MEN IN BLACK II

D) I, ROBOT

26) WHAT WAS THE NAME OF THE FIRST SUCCESSFUL ARTIFICIAL HEART IMPLANTED IN A HUMAN IN 1982?

A) JARVIK-7

B) ABIOCOR

C) SYNCARDIA

D) HEARTMATE

27) WHICH ICONIC EARLY 2000S TV SHOW FEATURED A GROUP OF FRIENDS LIVING IN PASADENA, CALIFORNIA, AND EXPLORING VARIOUS SCIENTIFIC TOPICS?

A) FRIENDS

B) HOW I MET YOUR MOTHER

C) THE BIG BANG THEORY

D) GILMORE GIRLS

28) WHO WAS THE FAMOUS SINGER KNOWN AS THE "QUEEN OF R&B" WHO ROSE TO FAME IN THE EARLY 2000S WITH HITS LIKE "UMBRELLA"?

A) AALIYAH

B) BEYONCÃ Â Ã Â©

C) ALICIA KEYS

D) RIHANNA

TIMELESS ✼ TRIVIA FOR ✼ SENIORS

29) WHAT WAS THE NAME OF THE FIRST SUCCESSFUL HEART TRANSPLANT, PERFORMED IN 1967?

A) BARNARD
B) DEBAKEY
C) COOLEY
D) SHUMWAY

30) WHICH ICONIC EARLY 2000S TV SHOW FEATURED A GROUP OF FRIENDS LIVING IN NEW YORK CITY AND EXPLORING DIFFERENT ROMANTIC RELATIONSHIPS?

A) FRIENDS
B) HOW I MET YOUR MOTHER
C) THE BIG BANG THEORY
D) SEX AND THE CITY

31) WHO WAS THE FAMOUS SINGER KNOWN AS THE "QUEEN OF POP" WHO ROSE TO FAME IN THE LATE 1990S AND CONTINUED HER SUCCESS IN THE EARLY 2000S?

A) CHRISTINA AGUILERA
B) MADONNA LOUISE CICCONE
C) ALICIA KEYS
D) BEYONCÃ Â Ã Â©

32) WHICH ICONIC EARLY 2000S FILM STARRED SHIA LABEOUF AS A YOUNG MAN WHO BECOMES A DRIVER FOR A SPY?

A) TRANSFORMERS
B) EAGLE EYE
C) DISTURBIA
D) INDIANA JONES AND THE KINGDOM OF THE CRYSTAL SKULL

TIMELESS ✻ TRIVIA FOR ✻ SENIORS

| SENIORS TRIVIA EDITION | **Nostalgic Trivia** | PAGE NO. 74 |

33) WHICH ICONIC EARLY 2000S TV SHOW FEATURED A GROUP OF FRIENDS LIVING IN NEW YORK CITY AND EXPLORING DIFFERENT ROMANTIC RELATIONSHIPS?

A) FRIENDS
B) HOW I MET YOUR MOTHER
C) THE BIG BANG THEORY
D) SEX AND THE CITY

34) WHO WAS THE FAMOUS SINGER KNOWN AS THE "PRINCESS OF R&B" WHO ROSE TO FAME IN THE EARLY 2000S WITH HITS LIKE "CRAVING YOU"?

A) AALIYAH
B) BEYONCÃ Â Ã Â©
C) ALICIA KEYS
D) RIHANNA

35) WHICH ICONIC EARLY 2000S FILM STARRED TOM HANKS AS A MAN STRANDED ON A DESERTED ISLAND AFTER A PLANE CRASH?

A) CAST AWAY
B) THE TERMINAL
C) CATCH ME IF YOU CAN
D) THE DA VINCI CODE

36) WHAT WAS THE NAME OF THE FIRST SUCCESSFUL KIDNEY TRANSPLANT, PERFORMED IN 1954?

A) MURRAY
B) STARZL
C) BARNARD
D) HARDY

TIMELESS ✱ TRIVIA FOR ✱ SENIORS

Nostalgic Trivia

SENIORS TRIVIA EDITION

PAGE NO. 75

37) WHO WAS THE FAMOUS SINGER KNOWN AS THE "QUEEN OF POP" WHO ROSE TO FAME IN THE LATE 1990S AND CONTINUED HER SUCCESS IN THE EARLY 2000S?

A) CHRISTINA AGUILERA

B) BRITNEY SPEARS

C) JESSICA SIMPSON

D) MANDY MOORE

38) WHICH ICONIC EARLY 2000S FILM STARRED ELIJAH WOOD AS A HOBBIT WHO EMBARKS ON A QUEST TO DESTROY AN EVIL RING?

A) THE LORD OF THE RINGS: THE FELLOWSHIP OF THE RING

B) THE LORD OF THE RINGS: THE TWO TOWERS

C) THE LORD OF THE RINGS: THE RETURN OF THE KING

D) THE HOBBIT: AN UNEXPECTED JOURNEY

39) WHAT WAS THE NAME OF THE FIRST SUCCESSFUL ARTIFICIAL HEART VALVE, DEVELOPED IN 1960?

A) STARR-EDWARDS

B) ST. JUDE MEDICAL

C) MEDTRONIC

D) EDWARDS LIFESCIENCES

40) WHICH ICONIC EARLY 2000S TV SHOW FEATURED A GROUP OF FRIENDS LIVING IN NEW YORK CITY AND EXPLORING DIFFERENT ROMANTIC RELATIONSHIPS?

A) FRIENDS

B) HOW I MET YOUR MOTHER

C) THE BIG BANG THEORY

D) SEX AND THE CITY

TIMELESS ✷ TRIVIA FOR ✷ SENIORS

Nostalgic Trivia

SENIORS TRIVIA EDITION

41) WHICH ICONIC EARLY 2000S FILM STARRED TOM HANKS AS A MAN STRANDED ON A DESERTED ISLAND?

A) CAST AWAY

B) THE TERMINAL

C) CATCH ME IF YOU CAN

D) THE DA VINCI CODE

42) WHAT WAS THE NAME OF THE FIRST SUCCESSFUL HEART-LUNG TRANSPLANT, PERFORMED IN 1981?

A) SHUMWAY

B) COOPER

C) BARNARD

D) STARZL

43) WHICH ICONIC EARLY 2000S TV SHOW FEATURED A GROUP OF FRIENDS LIVING IN NEW YORK CITY AND EXPLORING DIFFERENT ROMANTIC RELATIONSHIPS?

A) FRIENDS

B) HOW I MET YOUR MOTHER

C) THE BIG BANG THEORY

D) SEX AND THE CITY

44) WHO WAS THE FAMOUS SINGER KNOWN AS THE "QUEEN OF POP" WHO ROSE TO FAME IN THE LATE 1990S AND CONTINUED HER SUCCESS IN THE EARLY 2000S?

A) CHRISTINA AGUILERA

B) BRITNEY SPEARS

C) JESSICA SIMPSON

D) MANDY MOORE

TIMELESS ✶ TRIVIA FOR ✶ SENIORS

Nostalgic Trivia

SENIORS TRIVIA EDITION

45) WHAT WAS THE NAME OF THE FIRST SUCCESSFUL LIVER TRANSPLANT, PERFORMED IN 1963?

A) STARZL

B) MURRAY

C) BARNARD

D) DEBAKEY

46) WHICH ICONIC EARLY 2000S TV SHOW FEATURED A GROUP OF FRIENDS LIVING IN NEW YORK CITY AND EXPLORING DIFFERENT ROMANTIC RELATIONSHIPS?

A) FRIENDS

B) HOW I MET YOUR MOTHER

C) THE BIG BANG THEORY

D) SEX AND THE CITY

47) WHO WAS THE FAMOUS SINGER KNOWN AS THE "PRINCESS OF POP" WHO ROSE TO FAME IN THE LATE 1990S AND CONTINUED HER SUCCESS IN THE EARLY 2000S?

A) CHRISTINA AGUILERA

B) BRITNEY SPEARS

C) JESSICA SIMPSON

D) MANDY MOORE

48) WHICH ICONIC EARLY 2000S FILM STARRED NATALIE PORTMAN AS A YOUNG WOMAN WHO BECOMES A SKILLED BALLERINA WITH A DARK SIDE?

A) BLACK SWAN

B) THE WRESTLER

C) REQUIEM FOR A DREAM

D) THE FOUNTAIN

TIMELESS ✹ TRIVIA FOR ✹ SENIORS

SENIORS TRIVIA EDITION

Nostalgic Trivia

49) WHICH ICONIC EARLY 2000S TV SHOW FEATURED A GROUP OF FRIENDS LIVING IN NEW YORK CITY AND EXPLORING DIFFERENT ROMANTIC RELATIONSHIPS?

A) FRIENDS
B) HOW I MET YOUR MOTHER
C) THE BIG BANG THEORY
D) SEX AND THE CITY

50) WHO WAS THE FAMOUS SINGER KNOWN AS THE "QUEEN OF R&B" WHO ROSE TO FAME IN THE EARLY 2000S WITH HITS LIKE "CRAZY IN LOVE"?

A) AALIYAH
B) BEYONCÃ Â Ã Â©
C) ALICIA KEYS
D) RIHANNA

51) WHICH ICONIC EARLY 2000S FILM STARRED LEONARDO DICAPRIO AND TOM HANKS AS A TEAM OF INVESTIGATORS TRYING TO CATCH A SERIAL KILLER?

A) CATCH ME IF YOU CAN
B) THE DEPARTED
C) SHUTTER ISLAND
D) INCEPTION

52) WHAT WAS THE NAME OF THE FIRST SUCCESSFUL LUNG TRANSPLANT, PERFORMED IN 1963?

A) HARDY
B) COOPER
C) BARNARD
D) STARZL

TIMELESS ✶ TRIVIA FOR ✶ SENIORS

Answers

CHAPTER 1

1. C	2. B	3. D	4. A
5. C	6. B	7. B	8. A
9. B	10. C	11. A	12. A
13. C	14. C	15. C	16. A
17. C	18. C	19. A	20. B
21. D	22. D	23. B	24. A
25. B	26. C	27. B	28. B
29. C	30. B	31. A	32. A
33. C	34. B	35. A	36. C
37. D	38. A	39. B	40. B
41. C	42. B	43. A	44. D
45. A	46. A	47. C	48. A
49. D	50. B	51. A	52. D

CHAPTER 2

1. D	2. A	3. A	4. B
5. B	6. A	7. A	8. B
9. C	10. A	11. A	12. A
13. A	14. C	15. A	16. A
17. C	18. B	19. A	20. A
21. A	22. A	23. A	24. A
25. C	26. A	27. C	28. D
29. B	30. A	31. A	32. B
33. C	34. B	35. A	36. A
37. B	38. A	39. A	40. B
41. A	42. A	43. A	44. B
45. B	46. A	47. B	48. A
49. B	50. A	51. A	52. A

TIMELESS ✳ TRIVIA FOR ✳ SENIORS

Answers

CHAPTER 3

1.A	2.C	3.C	4.A
5.A	6.A	7.A	8.C
9.C	10.B	11.A	12.D
13.A	14.A	15.A	16.A
17.A	18.A	19.A	20.A
21.A	22.D	23.A	24.A
25.A	26.A	27.A	28.A
29.A	30.A	31.D	32.A
33.A	34.A	35.D	36.A
37.A	38.A	39.A	40.A
41.A	42.A	43.A	44.A
45.A	46.A	47.A	48.D
49.A	50.A	51.A	52.A

CHAPTER 4

1.A	2.C	3.A	4.A
5.A	6.D	7.A	8.D
9.B	10.B	11.B	12.A
13.A	14.A	15.B	16.C
17.A	18.A	19.A	20.A
21.C	22.A	23.A	24.A
25.A	26.A	27.A	28.A
29.A	30.A	31.A	32.C
33.C	34.A	35.B	36.B
37.B	38.A	39.A	40.C
41.A	42.A	43.A	44.C
45.A	46.A	47.D	48.B
49.A	50.A	51.C	52.A

TIMELESS ✷ TRIVIA FOR ✷ SENIORS

CHAPTER 5

1. B	2. C	3. A	4. A
5. B	6. A	7. B	8. D
9. A	10. A	11. D	12. C
13. A	14. B	15. D	16. A
17. B	18. A	19. C	20. A
21. B	22. B	23. A	24. D
25. A	26. A	27. C	28. D
29. A	30. B	31. B	32. A
33. B	34. D	35. A	36. A
37. B	38. C	39. A	40. D
41. A	42. A	43. D	44. B
45. A	46. D	47. C	48. A
49. B	50. D	51. A	52. B

CHAPTER 6

1. A	2. B	3. A	4. A
5. B	6. A	7. B	8. D
9. A	10. A	11. D	12. B
13. A	14. B	15. A	16. A
17. A	18. C	19. A	20. A
21. C	22. A	23. A	24. D
25. A	26. A	27. C	28. D
29. A	30. D	31. B	32. A
33. D	34. A	35. A	36. A
37. A	38. A	39. A	40. D
41. A	42. A	43. D	44. A
45. A	46. D	47. B	48. A
49. D	50. B	51. A	52. A

TIMELESS ✳ TRIVIA FOR ✳ SENIORS

Conclusion

THANK YOU FOR JOURNEYING THROUGH THE DECADES WITH TIMELESS TRIVIA FOR SENIORS: 312 MULTIPLE-CHOICE TRIVIA QUESTIONS FOR SENIORS TO RELIVE THE ICONIC 50S-00S ERAS.

WE HOPE THIS BOOK HAS SPARKED CHERISHED MEMORIES AND PROVIDED HOURS OF ENJOYMENT. WHETHER YOU'VE BEEN REMINISCING ALONE OR SHARING THESE MOMENTS WITH FRIENDS AND FAMILY, WE TRUST IT HAS BEEN A DELIGHTFUL EXPERIENCE.

FOR EVEN MORE FASCINATING TRIVIA AND NOSTALGIC FUN, BE SURE TO SCAN THE QR CODE ON THE BACK COVER. DISCOVER ADDITIONAL TITLES BY MASTER BOOKS AND CONTINUE YOUR TRIP DOWN MEMORY LANE. HAPPY REMINISCING!

THANK YOU
   - FACTS MASTER

TIMELESS ✻ TRIVIA FOR ✻ SENIORS

Notes

Date :

Notes

Date:

Notes

Date:

Printed in Great Britain
by Amazon